THE END OF THE HOLOCAUST: THE LIBERATION OF THE CAMPS

THE END OF THE HOLOCAUST:

THE LIBERATION OF THE CAMPS

Jon Bridgman

Richard H. Jones, Ph.D., General Editor

AREOPAGITICA PRESS
Portland, Oregon

Areopagitica Press
9999 S.W. Wilshire
Portland, Oregon 97225

Library of Congress Cataloging-in-Publication Data

Bridgman, Jon.
    The end of the Holocaust : the liberation of the camps / Jon
Bridgman ; Richard H. Jones, general editor.
        p.   cm.
    Bibliography: p.
    Includes index.
    ISBN 0-918400-12-0
    1. World War, 1939-1945--Concentration camps--Europe. 2. World
War, 1939-1945--Prisoners and prisons, German.   I. Jones, Richard
H. (Richard Hutton), 1914-   . II. Title.
D802.A2B72 1990
940.53'17--dc20   89-35704
                                                          CIP

TABLE OF CONTENTS

ACKNOWLEDGMENTS

The author wishes to thank Harper & Row, Publisher, Inc., for permission to quote from Michael Selzer, *Deliverance Day: The Last Hourse of Dachau;* Farrar Straus & Giroux, Inc., for permission to quote from Eugen Kogon, *The Theory and Practice of Hell* and Elie Wiesel, *Night;* Duckworth Press for permission to quote from Derrick Sington, *Belsen Uncovered;* the University of New Mexico Press for permission to quote from Marcus Smith, *Dachau, The Harrowing Hell;* and Stein and Day Publishers for permission to quote from Filip Müller, *Eyewitness Auschwitz.*

He also wishes to thank Mr. Kevin Mahoney who was responsible for obtaining the illustrations (all of which are reproduced courtesy of the National Archives).

INTRODUCTION

The liberation of the Nazi concentration camps has not been the sub-ject of much scholarly attention. Yehuda Bauer in an article entitled "Trends in Holocaust Research" (1979) lists a number of subjects which have attracted the interest of Holocaust scholars, but, not suprisingly, "liberation" is not mentioned.[1] At first glance, this seems quite under-standable: liberation, after all, was something like VE-Day, a dramatic moment to be sure, but hardly one that raises any questions of historical interest. The liberation of one camp was pretty much the same as the liberation of another: the Allied forces approached, the SS left, the tanks burst through the gates and the inmates were free. The actors in the drama reacted as one might expect! The liberating soldiers were at once horrified, angry, incredulous and deeply moved by what they saw; the inmates—or at least those with enough strength to react—were deliriously happy; and the guards were nowhere to be seen. There were no real surprises; very little needs to be explained. Liberation might be a fit subject for a *Life* pictorial essay, but hardly the subject for serious history. Conceivably a case could be made that had the Allied armies acted differently liberation might have been accomplished a few days sooner with the result that some additional lives would have been saved, but no one has made the case and there is little reason to do so. The Allied armies acted in good faith and with considerable expedi-tion. Liberation, then, is one aspect of the Holocaust to which the word "joyous" might properly be applied, and joyous events are rarely the stuff of history.

The drama of liberation, however, is somewhat more interesting historically if one considers not simply that brief, shining moment when the liberators burst into the camps and declared the inmates free, but rather that period of time extending from some weeks before the arrival of the liberators to a like period after. When viewed in this way liberation can be conveniently divided into three periods each with its own characteristics. First, the pre-liberation period extending from January to April 1945; second, the liberation proper;[2] and finally the post-liberation period ending in August 1945.

The pre-liberation period was characterized by a gradual alteration in the relationship of the prisoners and the SS. During these last months the authority of the SS gradually waned while the power of the inmates increased so that during the final days in most camps it was not altogether clear just where authority resided.[3] The waning of the authority of SS officials was largely due to the growing confusion at the highest levels of the National Socialist government as to whether all of the inmates in the camps, and Jews in particular, should be exterminated to prevent them from falling into the hands of the Allies or whether the lives of the survivors should be used as bargaining chips to get better terms for the Germans. Hitler, consistent to the end, held doggedly to the proposition that the elimination of world Jewry was a goal of such importance that it should take precedence over everything else; Himmler, on the other hand, wavered and finally broke with Hitler on this issue.[4] This confusion at the top was reflected in the orders given to the commandants of the camps, orders which were often contradictory and rarely gave the commandants unambiguous guidelines. The growing uncertainty among at least some of the SS officers emboldened resistance groups to take an ever stronger line against the orders of their masters which undoubtedly saved some lives, but the declining authority of the SS was also indirectly responsible for the fearsome epidemics that swept through most of the camps in the last weeks before the end of the war.

The period which we have called "Liberation Proper" was a time of great reservoirs of goodwill on both sides. The former inmates were willing to obey the galling but necessary orders of the liberators and were, for the most part, patient and understanding with the first fumbling attempts of the combat troops to restore some measure of order in the camps. The liberators, for their part, were full of deep compassion for the survivors and listened to any and all requests of the camps' leaders even if they often could do little about them.

The third stage of liberation, the "Post-Liberation Period," saw a gradual erosion of patience on both sides. By the end of August 1945, 90 percent of the inmates had been repatriated. Those who returned home were grateful to the Allied armies and their home governments for the speed and efficiency with which this massive transfer of population had been accomplished. However, for the 10 percent who remained in the camps, mostly Jews, there was much less to be grateful for. They remained in the camps either because they had no homeland to which to return or because they—particularly the Polish Jews—feared for their lives if they did return. They felt that paradoxically they were "liberated but not free," and increasingly came to blame the Allies for their predicament. The Allied military authorities responsible for the camps were equally frustrated because they knew that any permanent solution to the refugee problem was political in nature and beyond their competence.[5] The terminal date for the liberation period then is that point when the responsibility for the former inmates ceased being a humanitarian and became a political question.

When viewed in this broader context, liberation can be categorized by four different types. First, there was what might be called "Classic Liberation," that is, the sort of thing that happened at Bergen-Belsen. The camp was overrun by Allied forces and relief operations started almost at once. A second type is "Spontaneous Liberation." In most of the camps there was an underground organization which exerted some authority in the last hours before the arrival of the Allied armies, but only at Buchenwald did the inmates actually storm the guard towers and take complete control of the camp by the time the liberators arrived. A third form of liberation might be termed "Transfer Liberation" and it happened only once—at Theresienstadt. The SS authorities there transferred control of the camp to the International Red Cross which in turn turned control over to the Russians several days later. Finally, there is what we shall call—for want of a better term—"Hollow Liberation," which was exclusively confined to the East. The Red Army liberated many of the most infamous camps including Auschwitz, Majdanek, Sachsenhausen, etc., but in doing so they freed no more than a handful of prisoners. In each case evacuation had preceded the arrival of the Russians and there remained in the camps no more than a handful of prisoners too sick or weak to make the march to the West. Thus the advance of the Red Army, rather than signaling the end of the trial of the inmates of camps in the East, actually added to their agony.[6]

The manner in which the camps were liberated did have a minor impact on the immediate post-liberation period. Paradoxically, where there was a strong resistance movement, rescue operations were often impeded. This was particularly true at Buchenwald where the Communists—armed, healthy and well-fed—were in complete control when the liberators arrived. The Jews, or the majority of them, were for some time confined by the prisoner-guards in the notorious Little Camp, unfed and uncared for. At Bergen-Belsen, on the other hand, the British were able to act more expeditiously because they were not in any way inhibited by the prisoner organization for the simple reason that for all practical purposes such organization did not exist. But the point should not be pushed very far—the way in which the camps were liberated had only a small impact on what followed.

11

A second question is quite simply: "Who was liberated?" For historians of the Holocaust, "liberation" refers to the one hundred thousand or so Jews who survived the Final Solution that in the preceding four years had claimed six million lives. But Jewish inmates never accounted for more than a relatively small percentage of the total inmate population of the liberated camps; the bulk of the prisoners were common criminals, communists, gypsies, Seventh-Day Adventists, political prisoners, etc. Supreme Headquarters Allied Expeditionary Forces considered the camp inmates to be only a part of a much greater problem, namely that of Displaced Persons.[7] This designation included all civilians who were involuntarily resident in Germany. The military designated 11 categories of DPs: evacuees, war and political fugitives, political prisoners, forced and "voluntary" workers, Todt workers, deportees, civilian internees, ex-prisoners of war and stateless persons. In all, there were about 11 million DPs in Germany in addition to several million prisoners of war. Distinguished from DPs were "refugees," a designation for individuals who, while remaining in their own countries, had been forced by the Germans to re-locate for whatever reason. To handle this massive problem two organizations were set up: UNRRA, a civilian organization staffed by experts from all the Allied countries, and the Displaced Persons Executive (DPX), a military organization working out of Eisenhower's headquarters. Both DPX and UNRRA officials agreed to handle DPs in three stages: 1) free the DPs from any restraints; 2) transfer them to assembly centers; and 3) notify appropriate national authorities who would arrange for repatriation.

In general, it is fair to say that the policy was sound and carried out with remarkable expedition. Unfortunately for the Jews in the camps, less than one percent of the entire number of DPs, the policy had little relevance. (The same could be said for many of the Soviet nationals who were eventually repatriated by force.) The liberated Jews represented a unique problem because they had suffered more than any other group, and it was generally acknowledged that some special consideration should be shown to them for this reason. Further, unlike virtually all the other DPs, many Jews had no homeland to which to return, and no home government to assist in their repatriation. In particular, Lithuanian, Latvian and Estonian Jews, as well as the Jews who had lived in eastern Poland, had seen their homelands absorbed into the Soviet Union and thus these people were stateless. And finally, some Jews, Poles in particular, had good reason to fear for their lives if they returned to their former homes. By the end of August 1945, the overwhelming majority of the DPs had been repatriated, and only then were the Allied authorities brought face to face with the problem of Jewish survivors. Initially, the Allies had attempted to treat the Jews no differently from the other survivors but by the autumn of 1945 it was evident that such like treatment was neither morally acceptable nor politically feasible.

Genocide as such was ended in late 1944, but this did not end the appalling loss of life in the camps. Fully one-third of the Jews in the camps on January 1, 1945, died before liberation, and thousands more died in the first days after the arrival of the Allies. The reasons for this high loss of life are not in dispute. The deaths resulted from the policy of the National Socialist government: Jews were to be allowed to survive only if their survival was of some value to the German war effort. The victims died of over-work, starvation, disease, brutal treatment and random executions. Neither the reasons for the deaths nor the responsibility is at issue, but the fact that two-thirds survived raises questions. Hitler was determined that no Jew would survive the war, and in the SS he had a large number of fanatics who were perfectly willing to carry out his orders. Yet, against all odds, about 100,000 Jews were alive in the camps at the time of liberation. Why? First, some of the SS officers delegated to carry out the final extermination put their own personal safety above obedience to the orders of a collapsing regime and simply walked away. Second, in the last days of the war the Allied armies advanced so rapidly that they were able to frustrate plans for the annihilation of the surviving prisoners. Third, the inmates themselves in several camps were able to frustrate last-minute attempts to kill them. Fourth, various relief organizations, most notably the Swedish Red Cross, saved a number of inmates in the last days of the war. From February 19, 1945, until May 8, 1945, Count Folke Bernadotte and the Swedish Red Cross rescued 40,000 prisoners, many of them Jews.[8] On February 19, 1945, Bernadotte received permission from Himmler to assemble 13,000 Danish and Norwegian inmates at the Neugamme camp and put them under the control of the Red Cross. On April 15, 1945, Bernadotte arranged for the transfer of 830 Jews from Theresienstadt to safety. Five days later Himmler released 2,881 women from Ravensbrueck for transfer to Sweden. Three days thereafter another 11,700 women were released by Himmler, and on the last day of the war a further 10,000 were turned over to the Swedish authorities. Finally, another reason can explain why 100,0000 survived: those still alive in April 1945 were tough, resourceful, had an enormous will to live, and/or were lucky.

The post-liberation period was not characterized by any significant attempt on the part of the inmates to extract vengeance from their tormentors in particular, or the German people in general. There were, of course, isolated incidents, but they are remarkably few when one considers the magnitude of the suffering that the inmates had endured. The German people quite justifiably dreaded the day when the victims of the regime were finally free, but in fact when that day finally came very little happened. Those directly responsible for the crimes were in most cases given fair trials, and those only tangentially responsible rarely paid any penalty at all. Why was there no outburst of violence as all the pent-up hatred of years was finally released? The answer is partly to be found in the policy of the Allied armed forces which moved quickly to gain firm control of the camps, even using force in a few instances. But the answer is also to be found in the psychology of the survivors who tended to interpret the Holocaust in such a way that mindless vengeance seemed somehow inappropriate. A major of the Palestinian Brigade addressing a group of survivors in May 1945 exhorted them to "Unite! Be organized and disciplined!" That cry became in a sense the watchword of the survivors. The inmates demanded justice, indeed the whole world demanded justice, but in a "planet loaded with corpses" drumhead courts martial seemed somehow out of place.

Finally, the drama of liberation more than any other aspect of the Holocaust imprinted on the Western consciousness the images which have come to characterize the Final Solution. In a moral sense this proved to be of great importance since it ended once and for all the comforting belief, still widely held in the spring of 1945, that the atrocity stories were greatly exaggerated by Allied propagandists. After the liberation of the camps such beliefs lost their currency except among a true lunatic fringe. There has been no serious revisionism advanced relative to the *fact* of the Final Solution and the graphic evidence provided by liberation is partly responsible for this. That same graphic evidence, however, has led to a number of misconceptions which are still held by otherwise informed people. First, there was and is some confusion about the distinction between extermination camps and concentration camps. The sickening pictures of Bergen-Belsen with 13,000 unburied corpses were taken to be the ultimate horror while, in fact, Bergen-Belsen was a relatively mild camp, actually designated as a rest and recuperation center, and not to be compared to Auschwitz in terms of number of deaths. Furthermore, since Bergen-Belsen contained so many Jews it is often believed that those liberated were mostly Jews, whereas Jews were only a small fraction of the inmates of the liberated camps. Ninety-five percent of the Jews who came into the clutches of the SS were dead by May 1945. Finally, the chaotic disorder of many of the camps at the time of liberation was not at all typical. The horror of the camps until the last weeks was at least well organized. These misconceptions and others would be of little moment except that in recent years they have provided a thin wedge with which a handful of revisionists are attempting to discredit the facts of the Final Solution.[9]

In sum, the story of liberation presents some interesting historical problems. I believe the story is best approached as narrative history.

1. In *Essays on Holocaust History* (Jerusalem, 1979).
2. The dates of the liberation of the Western camps are:

Buchenwald	April 11, 1945
Bergen-Belsen	April 15, 1945
Dachau	April 29, 1945
Theresienstadt	May 7, 1945
Mauthausen	May 8, 1945

3. See Livia Rothkirchen, "The Final Solution in its Last Stages," *Yad Vashem Studies,* Volume VIII; Raul Hilberg, *The Destruction of the European Jews* (Chicago, 1961); Gerald Reitlinger, *The Final Solution: The Attempt to Exterminate the Jews of Europe, 1939–1945* (New York, 1953).
4. See Count Folke Bernadotte, *The Curtain Falls* (New York, 1945); Felix Kersten, *The Memoirs of Felix Kersten* (New York, 1947).
5. See Yehuda Bauer, "The Initial Organization of the Holocaust Survivors," in *Yad Vashem Studies,* Volume III. Bauer begins his article with the statement, "The epic of the Holocaust survivors in liberated Europe in the years 1945–1947 has been neglected by the historians of the period."
6. There is no detailed, scholarly account of the death marches, even though the whole episode reveals important aspects of the National Socialist regime in its dying days.
7. See Malcolm Proudfoot, *European Refugees* (Evanston, Illinois, 1956).
8. See Meir Dworzeck, "The International Red Cross and its Policy *vis-à-vis* the Jews in the Ghettos and the Concentration Camps in Nazi-Occupied Europe," in *Proceedings of the Second Yad Vashem International Conference Jerusalem, April 8–11, 1974: Rescue Attempts during the Holocaust.*
9. See Dr. Wilhelm Stäglich, *Der Auschwitz-Mythos* (Tübingen, 1979).

THE LIBERATION OF THE EASTERN CAMPS

Introduction

The Red Army liberated more camps than did the armies of the Western Allies and did so much earlier,[1] but in terms of the actual number of prisoners freed, the Russians accounted for no more than a small percentage. The reason for this anomaly is the simple fact that as the Russians advanced, the Germans, determined to prevent any prisoners from falling into the hands of the enemy, evacuated the camps and took the prisoners to the West. The only prisoners who remained were those too sick or too weak to make the march to the West.[2] The Russians' "liberations," then, led not to the freeing of the prisoners but rather to the death marches of the winter of 1944–1945 followed by the catastrophic over-crowding of the Western camps and the consequent epidemics which took the lives of tens of thousands of prisoners.

Although the Russian advance did not free more than a handful of the total camp population, it did provide unambiguous physical evidence of the reality of the Final Solution. But even after the first liberation of an extermination camp, Majdanek, in July 1944, a remarkably high percentage of the people in the West remained skeptical, dismissing eye-witness accounts and photographs as "Russian propaganda."[3] It was not until the liberation of Dachau, Mauthausen, Buchenwald, and above all Bergen-Belsen that the skeptics finally and unequivocally acknowledged that the Russian accounts were accurate. The truth about the camps was, if anything, worse than the most extreme rumors.

17

The Liberation of Majdanek

Until July 1944, the evidence that the Germans were systematically annihilating European Jewry was still largely circumstantial; that is not to say that a highly persuasive case had not been made, but the fact remained that skeptics could and did still argue that unambiguous physical evidence (the bodies, if you like) was lacking. That evidence was provided by the Russians in July 1944. On July 18, 1944, the Red Army launched a powerful offensive against the German forces in southern Poland. Deploying an enormous array of tanks, guns, and planes, the Russians shattered the German lines in the vicinity of Kowel. Long columns of the defeated Germans plodded to the West to try to re-establish their line along the Vistula with the Russians in hot pursuit. On July 23, only five days after the initial breakthrough, the Russian Second Tank Army by-passed Lublin and headed off in a northeasterly direction toward Warsaw. A few hours later infantry of the Eighth Guards Army, commanded by General Chuikov, took the town of Lublin itself. A short distance from the town they discovered the Majdanek concentration camp, the first of the infamous camps to be liberated.

Majdanek had been constructed in 1941 and consisted of 144 barracks, each designed to hold 300 prisoners, all enclosed behind a high, electrified, barbed wire fence.[4] When first opened, the camp had housed mostly prisoners of war and political prisoners, but by 1942 the camp had increasingly been used as an extermination camp for Polish Jews. Some were killed out of hand; others worked until they died. In all, about 400,000 prisoners, most of them Jews, died at Majdanek. At maximum capacity the camp held 40,000 prisoners, and there were as many more prisoners at six subsidiary camps: Blizn, Budesyn, Radom, Warsaw, and Lublin I and II. The Germans themselves called Majdanek a "Vernichtungslager (extermination camp)."[5] Heinz Stalbe, a member of the Kamppolizei, when questioned by the Polish and Soviet Extraordinary Committee that investigated Majdanek after liberation stated baldly: "The main purpose of the camp was to exterminate the greatest possible number of people, and for that reason it was called the Vernichtungslager."[6]

As early as April 1943 the Germans began to ship some of the Majdanek inmates to Auschwitz. When the Russians broke through on July 18, 1944, the SS moved rapidly to complete the evacuation, but their attempt was only partly successful. The prisoners organized in the Political Resistance Committee forced the Germans to leave several hundred of the inmates behind.[7] When the Russians reached the camp they found 1,000 "living skeletons." They also located six low-level camp functionaries who lacked either the wit or the means to flee to the West. For the most part those liberated were Polish or Russian prisoners of war, the Jews having long since been evacuated to Auschwitz. Chuikov ordered his soldiers to be escorted through the camp so that they might have the character of their enemy indelibly imprinted on their minds.[8] (Stalin's camps apparently were considered to be of another sort.) Chuikov reported that his men were less impressed by the gas chambers and instruments of torture than by the "storehouses of clothing stripped from children and old men and women who had been done to death there." In Lublin itself was a five-story warehouse, called the Chopin-Lager because it happened to be located on a street named after the composer, in which the possessions of the victims were stored. Here were cavernous rooms filled with suitcases, women's coats, razors, shoes, and even children's toys. Scattered on the floor of the Accounts Department of the Chopin-Lager were records the fast-departing German officials had failed to destroy. One letter contained a request for various items needed by 2,000 German school children who were being sent from their homes in the city to the safety of the countryside. Among other items requested were "sport shirts, training suits, coats, aprons, gym shoes, skiing boots, plus fours, warm underwear, warm gloves, and woolen scarves." In the last months before the arrival of the Russians the Chopin-Lager had shipped 18 fully loaded boxcars of goods to Germany.[9]

Chuikov not only had his own men escorted through Majdanek, he also forced German prisoners to take a tour of the camp. The Germans had to pass through ranks of jeering Poles. One old Jew (how he happened to survive is not recorded) chanted over and over again: "Kindermörder! Kindermörder (child murderers!)!"[10]

The Russians and the Poles set up a joint committee to investigate the crimes committed at Majdanek.[11] They interviewed dozens of survivors and also acted as a tribunal to try the six camp officials who had been apprehended—four Germans, three of them SS men, and two Poles. The committee concluded that 1.5 million men, women, and children had been killed or died at Majdanek. That figure is generally thought to be about three times too great, but at least it was in the right order of magnitude and correctly indicated the scale of the crimes being committed by the National Socialist regime.

The Soviet government, for reasons of its own, decided to give very wide press coverage to the story of Majdanek not only in the USSR but in the West as well. The first story from the camp was filed by Konstantin Simonov, the author of the immensely popular poem "Wait for Me," which had made his name a household word in Russia. It was hardly an accident that such a well-known figure was chosen to write the first story from the camp. His report, published in *Pravda*, had, according to a British correspondent in Moscow, "a shattering effect."[12] The Simonov article was followed by one written by Roman Karman, also a well-known correspondent. Karman wrote:

In the course of my travels into liberated territory I have never seen a more abominable sight than Majdanek near Lublin, Hitler's notorious *Vernichtungslager,* where more than half a million European men, women, and children were massacred . . . This is not a concentration camp; it is a gigantic murder plant.

Save for the 1,000 living corpses the Red Army found alive when it entered, no inmate escaped alive. Yet full trains daily brought thousands from all parts of Europe to be coldly, brutally massacred.

In the center of the camp stands a huge stone building with a factory chimney—the world's biggest crematorium. . . . The gas chambers contained some 250 people at a time. They were closely packed . . . so that after they suffocated they remainded standing . . . It is difficult to believe it myself but human eyes cannot deceive me . . .[13]

Karman also made a newsreel of the camp which was eventually shown in the West.[14]

The Soviet authorities also allowed two Western correspondents into Majdanek, first being H. W. Lawrence for the *New York Times.* His long, graphic account of the camp began with the justly famous lead: "I have just seen the most terrible place on the face of the earth."[15] The day after Lawrence's piece appeared the editors of the *Times* in an editorial on Majdanek assured their readers that Lawrence was a careful journalist, not given to overstatements. The editorial ended with a plea to the rival Polish factions to cease their squabbling because, after Majdanek, it was clear that "civilization itself was on trial." The New York *Herald Tribune* ended its Majdanek story with a warning that "maybe we should wait for further corroboration of the horror story that has come from Lublin. Even on top of all we have been taught of the maniacal Nazi ruthlessness, this tale sounds inconceivable . . ."[16] The second Western correspondent admitted to Majdanek was Alexander Werth, an Englishman who had lived in Russia up to the time of the revolution and had a well-known pro-Russian bias. He filed a story with the BBC but it was rejected as "a Russian propaganda stunt," or at least that was Werth's account of the matter. On September 18, 1944, his story finally appeared in the *Christian Science Monitor.*

In October the *Illustrated London News* published 12 pictures of the camp. The accompanying text is, in some ways, more provocative than the pictures.

It is not the custom of *The Illustrated London News* to publish photographs of atrocities, but in view of the fact that the enormity of the crimes perpetrated by the Germans is so wicked that our readers, to whom such behaviour is unbelievable, may think the reports of such crimes exaggerated or due to propaganda, we consider it necessary to present them, by means of the accompanying photographs, with irrefutable proof of the organized murder of between 600,000 and 1,000,000 helpless persons at the Majdanek Camp near Lublin. And even these pictures are carefully selected from a number, some of which are too horrible to reproduce ... The story as it stands is almost incredible in its bestiality, but German cruelty went further still at Majdanek. Prisoners too ill to walk into the camp ... were dragged alive to the furnaces and thrust in alongside the dead ... This camp, as it stands today is a grim reminder of that streak of utter inhumanity which is found in every German.[17]

Oddly enough, the publication of the stories and pictures from Majdanek had little impact on public opinion in the West. Those who believed were confirmed in their belief; those who did not believe remained skeptical. The story was given only moderate prominence in the Western press. In the popular mind the name Majdanek counted (and even today counts) for very little. In Germany, however, the liberation of Majdanek had a much greater impact. Reitlinger notes that "it is remarkable how many high-placed Germans said they were convinced of the truth of the gas chamber stories only after they read of the Allied revelations on Lublin . . ."[18] To Hans Frank, Governor-General of Poland from 1939 to 1945, the revelations of Majdanek were devastating. "Now we know," he whined to a subordinate. "You cannot deny that."[19] He comforted himself with the thought that though he could never claim ignorance after Majdanek, he could claim that the responsiblity for the camps was not his even though they were located in his bailiwick. At other times Frank accused the world press of defaming Germany with the horror stories from Majdanek. According to David Irving, Hitler airily dismissed the Majdanek story as the equivalent of the Allied propaganda stories of the First World War.[20]

In that same summer of 1944, the Russians also overran three extermination camps: Belzec, Sobibor, and Treblinka; yet they made no mention of these camps in their own press and none appeared in the Western press at the time. Belzec was opened on March 17, 1942. In the 18 months that the camp operated about 600,000 Jews were killed there. The camp was closed down in 1943. Before the Russians arrived Jewish workers were sent to Belzec to clean out the burial pits and burn the bodies. The Russians occupied the area in mid-1944 but perhaps did not immediately understand what had happened there.

The second camp overrun by the Russians in that summer was Sobibor. Here between May 8, 1942, and October 1943, between 250,000 and 600,000 Jews, Russians, Poles, and gypsies were killed. In October 1943, 600 prisoners overpowered the guards and escaped, of whom perhaps as many as 30 survived the war. Probably as a result of the revolt, Himmler ordered the camp closed down. All the permanent buildings were dynamited, large cranes excavated the burial pits, and the bodies were burned. To complete the concealment of the site, pine trees were planted where the camp had once been. As in the case of Belzec, the Russians reported nothing about Sobibor.

Finally, the Red Army came upon Treblinka. Here between 700,000 and 1,000,000 Warsaw Ghetto Jews were exterminated. Extermination at Treblinka had ceased in October 1943 and all the existing buildings had been blown up, the land plowed over and all other traces of the camp obliterated. There was a second, much smaller camp at Treblinka. It was a labor camp, and in all, only 10,000 prisoners passed through this camp, of whom 7,500 died. The Red Army liberated Treblinka II on July 24, 1944. Whether the Russians discovered the full magnitude of the horror of the Treblinka extermination camp is unclear, but at least they did not release at that time any details that found their way into the Western press. Thus when the summer ended, the Russians had liberated two camps (Treblinka II and Majdanek) and had by-passed three others (Belzec, Treblinka I and Sobibor).

In August, the Red Army came to a stop along the Vistula and remained there for the balance of the year. The Russians explained their immobility in purely military terms—the great advances made since early spring had stretched the lines of communication to the limit and time was needed to bring up reinforcements, consolidate positions, repair transportation facilities, and rest their exhausted troops. Cynics pointed out that the Russians, having encouraged the non-communist Polish Home Army to rise against the Germans, now watched passively while Hitler's troops destroyed the Poles, in effect acting as Stalin's executioners. During this lull, which lasted from August 1944 to January 1945, the Germans evacuated 27,000 Jews from subsidiary camps in the Warsaw area and sent them to Auschwitz.

The Liberation of Auschwitz

When the Russians resumed their offensive in January 1945, only two large camps remained east of the Oder River: Auschwitz-Birkenau and Stutthof. Though some preliminary steps had been taken to comply with Himmler's orders that in the future no living prisoners were to be left in the camp if it had to be abandoned to the enemy, for the most part the camps continued to operate almost to the end in their usual and accustomed patterns save for the closure of the gas chambers in October. For Auschwitz that meant that new inmates continued to be brought into the camp, the last transport arriving on January 5, 1945, and the random killing of Jews went on to the last day. During the summer and autumn the rate of extermination continued at a high level, averaging about 1,000 per day.[21] Sometime in September or October, according to an affidavit given by SS Standartenfuehrer Kurt Becher, Himmler ordered the end of the extermination policy. The order read:

I forbid any further annihilation of Jews and order instead proper care be given to the weak and the sick. I hold them [that is, Pohl and Kaltenbrunner] personally responsible if this order is not carried out by their subordinates.[22]

Himmler's motives were varied.[23] First, he believed that he might well emerge as the leading figure in postwar Germany if he could distance himself from the extermination policy of his government; second, he wanted to clear Germany's name which he knew would be "dishonored" by the excesses that occurred in the camps; finally, he almost certainly wanted to save his own skin by posing as the one man capable of stopping genocide even at this late hour. Himmler had reason to be nervous because the Allies were becoming ever sterner in their warnings to the Germans that a day of reckoning would soon be at hand. In early October, the Council for the Rescue of the Jewish Population in Poland warned both the British Foreign Office and the American State Department that the Germans were about to murder "all persons imprisoned in Auschwitz." The Council pleaded with the British and the Americans "to do everything possible" to prevent this catastrophe.[24] On October 19, 1944, a joint British-American warning was issued which was countered by a statement from the Germans that "these reports are false from beginning to end." On October 19, 1944, Professor Lindley Fraser, the leading BBC German-language news commentator gave the German people a further warning. "Let all other people concerned be warned: these atrocities are capital crimes."[25] On November 7, 1944, Eisenhower followed up with a warning of his own in the form of a leaflet dropped over Germany and entitled "Attention Germans!" containing the grim warning that the Allies "expected to find these persons [that is, inmates of the camps] alive and unharmed." What influence these various warnings had on Himmler is uncertain, but on November 26 he followed up his order ending genocide with instructions to the Auschwitz commandant to tear down the remaining crematoria, and added for good measure that henceforth Jews working in Germany were to receive the same rations as East European workers.[26] But Himmler no longer had sufficient control over his underlings to insure that his orders were strictly carried out. It is true that genocide in the form of mass gassings did end, but the slaughter of Jews in enormous numbers continued right up to the end of the war.

In July 1944, Auschwitz had a prison population of 135,000; by January 1945 this figure had dropped to 65,000—partly as a result of evacuation and partly due to the extremely high death rates in the camp even after gassings stopped in October 1944.[27] On January 12, 1945, the Russian central front which had been quiescent since August came to life. When the German line failed to hold, Hoess, the commandant of the camp, ordered the evacuation of Auschwitz-Birkenau with all possible speed.[28] On January 18, 1945, the last roll call was held. Of the

23

58,000 prisoners still in the camp, about 50,000 were considered physically capable of making the march to the West. That day and the next column after column marched out of the camp, some to nearby railheads where they were put into open cars for a journey that lasted days, sometimes weeks; others marched the whole distance. The following descriptions are by survivors.[29]

> The entire camp was in a turmoil of excitement, with prisoners seized by alarm and euphoria at one and the same time... Everywhere confusion was at its height. Then, before midnight, the order to march was given. It was an exhilarating moment. Outside it was snowing and very cold. Some 20,000 prisoners formed up in a long marching column and, flanked by SS guards, set out into the night. The snow crunched under our feet, a cold wind blew in our faces. We talked about nothing except where they were taking us and what they intended to do with us. We marched intermittently for a few days until we came to Loslau where we were herded into open railway cattle trucks. Many people did not survive this long march without hot food or drink and without warm clothes. The physically weak and sick lasted only a few hours. Anyone too exhausted to go on was shot by the guards.

Another description:

> When the Russians began to come close to Auschwitz the Germans began marching all prisoners who could walk right into Germany. It was January 1945 and we walked through the night in the cold and snow. We slept as we walked. We were five in a row and the man in the middle slept; then we would rotate and give someone else a chance to be carried.

Most of the inmates were taken to either Buchenwald (13,866), Sachsenhausen (19,905), Mauthausen (8,365), or Dachau (1,379). Eugen Kogon, who was at Buchenwald when the Auschwitz prisoners arrived wrote:

> In endless columns, the wretched host rolled over the countryside, day after day, often for weeks, without food and adequate clothing. Those who could not go further were shot down by the SS or their prisoner minions, or were simply left by the wayside ... The more centrally located camps had to make room for thousands upon thousands of evacuees who reported stories of unbelievable terror ... One had only to look at these wretched figures pouring into the narrowing interior from every side to believe them.[30]

By January 19, 1945, about 6,000 prisoners remained in Auschwitz-Birkenau, the majority because they were too feeble to make the march, with a few able-bodied men to take care of various clean-up details. Among other things huge stores of food were loaded on trains for shipment to Germany. The guards, who had once numbered 4,000 were now few in number and visibly "nervous and apprehensive." In the succeeding days the electrical system failed, the water supply was cut and the central heating was turned off.[31] An order to kill all the remaining prisoners was not carried out apparently because there were too few guards to accomplish it. Day after day, the prisoners saw large columns of defeated German soldiers streaming to the West as the sounds of Russian artillery grew louder and louder. On January 24, 1945, an inmate noted in his diary that the SS had "vanished into thin air." The next day, however, a 40-man SS patrol reappeared in Auschwitz and ordered the prisoners out of their barracks and into the *Appellplatz* (roll call area). Those who were still able to stand obeyed the order assuming that they were about to be executed. Their suspicions seemed to be confirmed by random shootings which were taking place throughout the camp. At the last moment, a messenger on a motorcycle appeared, gave a message to the SS commander, and then departed. The SS commander shouted: "Everyone back to the block." The actual message was not recorded, but a witness said that the SS "seemed more scared than we were" and hastily departed. A few hours later 1,500 inmates from Birkenau arrived reporting that earlier that day they had been ordered to form up and march to Auschwitz. Before they had gone halfway, a messenger on a motorcycle had talked to their guards and they too had disappeared. By January 27, 1945, the prisoners had the camp entirely to themselves. Russian artillery fire was very near and the survivors suspected that the day of liberation was at hand. In the middle of the afternoon of January 27, 1945, Auschwitz was liberated. From a prisoner's daybook one gets a graphic account of the actual moment.

> January 27th. A beautiful, sunny winter's day. During the morning all was calm and peaceful except for the strain of the long waiting. At about 3 P.M. we heard a noise in the direction of the main gate. We hurried to the scene. It was a Soviet forward patrol—Soviet soldiers in white caps! There was a mad rush to shake them by the hand and shout our gratitude. Several prisoners waved red scarves. The shouts of joy would have gone on forever had not the Soviet N.C.O. declared that the patrol had to be on its way again. They went off to the west. About an hour later, a larger body of Soviet troops arrived. They went through the blocks and the other buildings in the camp. They then set up their guard posts and gave us food. We were liberated!
>
> January 28th. The Soviet soldiers tended the sick with the utmost care; doctors and hospital orderlies battled to save each life. The total number of prisoners liberated at Auschwitz was 2,819, including 200 children aged from six to fourteen. Several hundred dead were given the first dignified funeral to be seen at Auschwitz.[32]

The Soviet soldiers who initially entered the camp were attached to the

First Perekop Division, a unit of the First Ukrainian Front; the commanding officer of the first troops in the camp was Colonel Gregory Dawidovicz Yelizabetskiy, a Russian Jew.[33] Apparently about half of the 6,000 prisoners the Germans left behind had died between January 19 and January 27, and the other 1,000 died in the next few days. The total number of Auschwitz survivors was less than 2,000, 95 percent of them Jews.

The liberation of Auschwitz was an incidental by-product of the Russian winter offensive. The main objective of that operation was Silesia—Stalin had pointed to this rich industrial region on a map and said laconically, "Gold!" A late-1944 attempt by the camp underground to sneak out five couriers carrying pleas for help to the Russians failed and the five were summarily executed. But had they succeeded in reaching the Russian lines there is no reason to believe that Stalin would have listened to their pleas for assistance. Stalin did not let humanitarian considerations influence his military decisions, and in any case he had little sympathy with prisoners of war (in late 1944 there were still large numbers of POWs in the camp), considering them cowards at best, traitors at worst.

After liberation a joint Polish and Russian investigating committee was set up to determine what exactly happened in Auschwitz during its four years of existence. To begin with, the commissioners stated that the Russian High Command only became aware of the existence of the extermination camp at Auschwitz a short time before liberation. On the face of it this statement seems false. The committee estimated that 4 million citizens of the Soviet Union, Poland, France, Czechoslovakia, Belgium, Holland, and other lands were put to death at Auschwitz. There followed a detailed description of the camp, its organization, the economic enterprises associated with it, the medical experiments done at the camp, the methods of killing, etc. The report was based largely on the testimony of some 2,000 survivors who were interviewed, and their testimony made up the bulk of the report. An accurate accounting was given of the loot found in the camp: Item, 348,820 men's suits; item, 836,255 women's coats and dresses; etc. The report also contained an statement signed by a number of former inmates appealing to the world to prevent such a thing as Auschwitz from happening again. The report is 20 pages long and there is not one mention in it of Jews or the fact that Auschwitz was the principal center for carrying out the Final Solution.[34]

For reasons that are not completely clear, the Soviet government not only did not give the publicity to the liberation of Auschwitz that it lavished on the liberation of Majdanek; indeed, it seemed determined to prevent the world from finding out anything about Auschwitz and what happened there. On February 15, 1945, the British Foreign Office asked the ambassador in Moscow to make inquiries about "what might have actually been discovered [at Auschwitz] since press reports suggest that the Soviet forces have recently liberated the so-called camp at Oswiecim." It was not until two months later that the Soviet Foreign Minister finally replied to the British note. He wrote that "it has been found from investigations from the Oswiecim group of concentration camps that more than 4,000,000 citizens of various European countries were destroyed by the Germans." The letter concluded with the afterthought that "no British were found among the survivors." The only English-language account of the camp appeared in *Polpress*, February 23, 1945. A Polish officer wrote that "Those who survive don't look like human beings, they are mere shadows." He also reported that the number of victims was so great "that the Germans found it impossible to burn all the bodies in stoves. They were obliged to burn them in bonfires." Finally, on May 7, 1945, the Russians published an account of the liberation of Auschwitz, but, of course, it was buried in the news of the unconditional surrender of Germany. The general public took almost no notice of the story, but a British Foreign Office official after reading the Russian account noted: "It is generally agreed that Oswiecim was the worst of all camps."

There was only one other sizable camp east of the Oder in the autumn of 1944, Stutthof, about 22 miles east of Danzig.[35] By 1944 Stutthof had come close to being an extermination camp, though technically it was a heavy labor camp. It had the dubious distinction of the highest death rate of any concentration camp. During the latter half of 1944 tens of thousand of Jews, mostly women, were taken to the camp, some from Hungary, some from Ostland and 20,000 from Auschwitz. In late January 1945, as the Russian armies were nearing the camp, the order was given to evacuate all those capable of making the march. Of the 40,000 in the camp, 35,000 were rated as march-capable. A survivor related what happened to her particular group.

> It was the last days of January 1945. The Germans had started the rumor that at the coast we'd be put on board a ship for Hamburg; we didn't believe it. We saw the pickets; a guard every five yards with a submachine gun pointed at us and the heavily guarded sleds, travelling constantly up and down the column. We didn't believe the evacuation story... Suddenly there was a terrific shouting coming from up front, where the men were marching. Flares flew up and illuminated the whole landscape. It was later that I heard that, at that moment, a group of 300 prisoners had gone for the SS with their bare hands. They were all shot... Then the rumor: The SS were driving us into the sea! This was true, we knew it at once. Where were the ships that were waiting for us then? We were not making for anywhere, no kind of bay where a big ship could anchor. Besides there were still over 8,000 of us... SS men with machine-guns stood on the rocks to the left and to the right of us. They drove the prisoners to the edge of the pre-

cipice and shot them down mercilessly. If anyone tried to turn back he was soon grabbed by the armed guards before he could manage a step.

This woman was one of the few survivors of the massacre. In all, only a few hundred of the 35,000 inmates of Stutthof reached the West alive. As it turned out, the camp itself was not actually liberated until two days after the end of the war. When the Russians arrived they found only a few German criminals and some regular soldiers.

As the Russian drive to the Vistula had led to the evacuation of Majdanek and its subsidiary camps, so the Russian drive to the Oder led to the evacuation of Auschwitz and Stutthof. The third and last great Russian offensive of the final phase of the war commenced on April 16, 1945, as the Red Army stormed over the Oder. Once again, the Germans evacuated the camps—in this case Gross Rosen, Sachsenhausen, and Ravensbrueck—before the Russians arrived. In February, Gross Rosen in Silesia was evacuated, the prisoners taken to Buchenwald. In April 1945, Sachsenhausen had over 50,000 inmates although it had provision to house no more than one-sixth that number. On February 2, 1945, Red Cross officials visited the camp and offered to put it under international supervision. Himmler was not adverse to the plan but Hitler vetoed it. Consequently, yet another death march took place. Forty thousand inmates were marched to the West while 3,000 sick and dying were left in the camp.[36]

On April 28, 1945, the same thing happened at Ravensbrueck, the only exclusively women's camp in the East. In April Himmler, through the good offices of his masseur Kersten, had entered into negotiations with Norbert Masur of the World Jewish Conference and Count Bernadotte.[37] These negotiations led to an agreement by which thousands of women were taken from Ravensbrueck to freedom. Among those saved were about 1,000 Jewish women. The remaining inmates were evacuated on April 28, 1945, so the Russians found only 3,000 dying prisoners when they reached the camp.

To summarize the results of the liberation of the Eastern camps:

Camp	Number Evacuated	Number Remaining In Camp	Destination
Majdanek	40,000	1,000	Auschwitz
Nebenlagern	37,000	0	Auschwitz
Auschwitz	65,000	3,000	Buchenwald, Mauthausen, Dachau, Sachsenhausen
Stutthof	35,000	2,000	Hamburg?
Sachsenhausen	40,000	3,000	—
Ravensbrueck	17,000	3,000	—
Gross Rosen	?	?	Buchenwald

Of the 250,000 prisoners in the Eastern camps, only 12,000 were liberated by the Russians, and many of those liberated died shortly thereafter. Of those evacuated about 100,000 survived to the end of the war, and those survivors accounted for the bulk of the Jews liberated in April–May 1945.

As the endless streams of evacuees poured into the Western camps putting ever greater strain on the crumbling administrative system, a disaster of major proportion impended. The Red Cross, various Jewish organizations, and Swiss and Swedish diplomats worked together to avoid the worst. Hitler opposed any rescue plan and indeed was determined that no Jew in his control would survive the war. General Oswald Pohl, the head of the Wirtschaftverwaltunghauptamt (head office of the Economic Administration of the SS, the agency responsible for administration of the camps) and Ernst Kaltenbrunner, the head of the Security Police and SD, remained fanatically loyal to the ideal of total extermination. Himmler, on the other hand, was for his own reasons quite willing to consider allowing the remaining inmates to pass under the control of one international agency or another. The upshot was that several thousand prisoners, most of whom would probably have died, were in fact saved in the last weeks of the war.

1. Camps liberated by the Russians
    Majdanek   July 23, 1944
    Belzec   July 1944 (Camp had been closed since 1943)
    Treblinka   July 25, 1944 (The extermination camp was closed
                      but a small concentration camp remained)
    Sobibor   July 1944 (Camp had been closed since 1943)
    Auschwitz   January 27, 1945
    Gross Rosen   February 1945
    Stutthof   May 10, 1945
    Sachsenhausen   April 1945
    Ravensbrueck   April 1945
    Theresienstadt   May 1945

    With the exception of Natzweiler, which was liberated in November 1944 after all inmates had been evacuated, the Allies did not liberate any camps until April 1945.
2. See accounts of individual camps for details.
3. On January 3, 1945, Captain D. McLaren of the British Psychological Warfare Division wrote: "The British and American people are still not as a whole willing to believe that the German atrocities . . . have been anything like they are . . ." He recommended that a special publication be prepared with photographs "setting forth the record of the Gestapo." The Head of the Political Intelligence Department, Ritchie Calder, approved McLaren's plan but he himself remained somewhat skeptical. See Martin Gilbert, *The Allies and Auschwitz*, p. 334.
4. For a description see Edward Gryn and Zofia Murowska, *Majdanek Concentration Camp* (Lublin, 1966).
5. Technically, of course, Majdanek was a "Work-Extermination Camp." The designation "Extermination Camp" was reserved for places like Treblinka, such a distinction is academic.
6. *Polish Black Book*, p. 381.
7. Kogon, *The Theory and Practice of Hell*, p. 247. There were practically no Jews in Majdanek at the time of liberation. The number of survivors is variously given as 6,000 (Kogon) and 1,000 (*The Polish Black Book*). The higher figure may refer to the survivors in the subsidiary camps.
8. Vasili Chuikov, *The End of the Third Reich* (London, 1967) p. 41.
9. Alexander Werth, *Russia at War* (New York, 1964) p. 897.
10. *Ibid.*, p. 896.
11. This report is printed in the *Polish Black Book*, pp. 381–390.
12. *Times* (London).
13. *Time*, August 21, 1944.
14. *New York Times*, April 28, 1945.
15. *Ibid.*
16. New York *Herald Tribune*, April 28, 1945.
17. *Illustrated London News*, October 14, 1944.
18. Reitlinger, p. 450.
19. Hilberg, p. 630.
20. Irving, *Hitler's War* (London, 1977). Irving says: "On October 17, 1944 news reports reached Hitler that the Russians claimed to have found a former concentration camp, Majdanek, near Lublin, at which 1,500,000 people were liquidated; according to Heinz Lorenz, his press officer, Hitler angrily

dismissed the reports as propaganda—just as German troops had been accused of "hacking off children's hands in Belgium" in 1914. When Ribbentrop pressed him for an answer, the Fuehrer replied reassuringly, "That is Himmler's affair and his alone." If this report is accurate, it is, to say the least, very revealing of a number of aspects of the regime.

21. In the month of October 1944, 33,000 were exterminated at Auschwitz and this despite the uprising of the Sonderkommando on October 17 in which one of the crematoriums was destroyed.
22. IMT Document 3762-PS.
23. There is no really satisfactory account of Himmler's part in all this. See Heinrich Fraenkel and Roger Manvell, *Himmler* (New York, 1965) and Achim Besgen, *Der Stille Befehl: Medizinalrat Kersten und das Dritte Reich* (Munich, 1966).
24. Ambassador Winant passed on the warning to the State Department.
25. Gilbert, p. 326.
26. Gilbert, p. 331; Hilberg, p. 631; Kastner, *Bericht*, p. 131; Reitlinger, p. 495.
27. On January 7, 1945 the number of Jews in Auschwitz was as follows:

Main Camp	16,000	
Birkenau	14,000	
Monowitz	35,000	
Total	65,000	(From Gilbert, p. 334)

28. Gilbert, p. 335; Hilberg, p. 632; Reitlinger, pp. 492 ff.
29. Filip Mueller, *Eyewitness Auschwitz* (1979) pp. 166 ff.
30. Eugen Kogon, *The Theory and Practice of Hell* (New York, 1958) pp. 273–274.
31. Primo Levi, *Survival in Auschwitz* (London, 1976) pp. 137 ff.
32. Petro Mirchuk, *In The German Mills Of Death* (New York, 1975) p. 268.
33. Reuben Ainsztein, *Jewish Resistance in Nazi-Occupied Eastern Europe* (New York, 1974) p. 816.
34. Jozef Garlinski, *Fighting Auschwitz: The Resistance Movement in the Concentration Camp* (Greenwich, Connecticut, 1975) pp. 312 ff.
35. See Konnilyn Feig, *Hitler's Death Camps* (New York, 1979) pp. 191–204.
36. See Livia Rothkirchen, "The Final solution in its Last Stages" in Gutman and Rothkirchen eds., *The Catastrophe of European Jewry* (Jerusalem, 1976).
37. See R. Hawkins, *Count Folke Bernadotte* (Minneapolis, Minnesota, 1950).

BERGEN-BELSEN

Introduction

The name Bergen-Belsen has come to symbolize the horrors of the Holocaust. The photographs of the camp littered with 13,000 bodies, the hollow-eyed, emaciated prisoners, the sleek and brutal-looking guards fixed indelibly on the Western consciousness the grim reality of the Final Solution.[1] So disturbing was the visual impact of the first pictures of Bergen-Belsen that the editors of the *Illustrated London News* felt impelled to put those pictures in a detachable four-page supplement "intended for our adult readers only. Our subscribers with young families whom they do not desire to see the photographs, can remove these pages . . ." (The editors of *Life* were not so solicitous of the feelings of their young readers.) Bergen-Belsen not only symbolized the Final Solution but also served to remove the last doubts about its reality. In an editorial in *Spectator* the meaning of Belsen was summarized as follows: "As long as there was any conceivable loop-hole of doubt many persons in this country dared to hope that there was at least exaggeration about the hideousness and the scale of atrocities committed in German concentration camps. Some doubts might have been dispelled by the records of Lidice and Lublin [it is noteworthy that Auschwitz was as yet barely known in the West], but if any still remains it must vanish forever in view of what was found at Buchenwald . . . Nordhausen and Belsen, perhaps the worst of all."[2] In June the British burned the camp to the ground. The editors of *Time* commented that the fire only destroyed the physical structure of the camp, not the impulse behind it.

> But more than fire was needed to destroy the causes that produced Belsen, for they lay deeper than any tendency to scientific brutality on the part of the German people. They lay in the

33

political philosophy of totalitarianism, which is not the exclusive property of any people. If this was understood, the thousands of men and women who died in anonymous agony at Belsen would not have died completely in vain. Failure to understand this meant that they would have died for absolutely nothing, that the meaning of Belsen would be dissipated in moral revulsion and invective, that other Belsens would recur in history. The meaning of Belsen was the ultimate meaning of all totalitarianism.[3]

The British tended to see Belsen less in cosmic terms and more in terms of crime and punishment. "This terrible degradation of humanity is the worst crime civilization can record throughout the ages and no punishment devised can offer sufficient retribution of these infamies," wrote one editor whose response was fairly typical. However the crimes of the National Socialists were interpreted, Belsen was the focal point of the discussion at least until the full magnitude of what happened in Eastern Europe came to be appreciated.

That Bergen-Belsen acquired this status is to some degree an historical accident. Had the camp been liberated six months before it surely would never have acquired its sinister reputation. Up to the beginning of 1945 Bergen-Belsen was mild compared to other camps in Germany. (One must emphasize, of course, that "mild" is used relatively and not absolutely.) But in the last weeks of the war Bergen-Belsen changed from a "model" camp to a nightmare which rivalled Dore's drawings of Dante's inferno. The story of the disaster at Belsen is complex, but some appreciation of what happened there in the last weeks is critical to understanding the impact that the liberation made in the West.

In all the contemporary accounts of the Bergen-Belsen liberation there are remarkably few references to Jews. In the case of the liberation of other camps this is partly understandable because Jews made up generally no more than 10 percent of the inmate population, but this is certainly not the case of Bergen-Belsen. There may have been as many as 40,000 Jews in the camp in the last days (some were removed just before liberation), which is somewhere between one-third and one-half of all the Jews who survived in the camps.[4] It is for this reason that the liberation of Belsen has an important place in any history of the Holocaust. Furthermore, in the five years that followed liberation the survivors, moved to the defunct SS Panzer Training School located two miles from the old camp, became the most important members of survivor culture in Europe. A community, almost a city, grew up and flourished there. One of the leaders of the community, Josef Rosensaft described the new Belsen as a shtetl (a small East European Jewish community): "Perhaps it was—the last shtetl in Europe, whose inhabitants teeter-tottering between despair and exhiliration, were suspended between past and future."[5]

The Origins of Bergen-Belsen

The origin of the concentration camp at Bergen-Belsen was completely unique; it bore no resemblance to the origins of any other camp. Belsen came into existence because of the diplomatic and political problem caused by the presence of foreign Jews in Germany. When the National Socialist Party came to power in 1933 there were 499,682 Jews in Germany, 20 percent of whom (98,747) were not German citizens. Of the latter group one-fifth (19,746) were stateless while the remainder held passports from a number of different states. The overwhelming majority of foreign Jews in Germany in 1933 were Poles (56,480). There were also substantial numbers of Austrians (4,647), including the famous theoretical physicist Lise Meitner; Czechs (4,275); Hungarians (2,280); Rumanians (2,210); and smaller numbers from other states including a few Americans.[6] Ideologically, of course, the National Socialists did not in any way differentiate these Jews from German Jews. To the Nazi a Jew was a Jew, a racial enemy of the German people, and this was true irrespective of legal technicalities like citizenship papers or passports.[7] But the German Foreign Office, sensitive as ever to the pressures of world public opinion, strongly urged the government to adopt the traditional attitude towards all foreigners residing in Germany.[8] To act otherwise courted the danger of retaliation.

In the early years of the regime this cautious policy was adopted officially (unofficially foreign Jews were often subjected to random terror of the SS and SA). When the government announced its first major anti-semitic action, the boycott of April 1, 1933, the *Völkische Beobachter* warned the "Action Committees" that they would be held accountable if any harm came to foreigners "regardless of race, creed or religion."[9] It was not until 1938 that the government overtly moved against foreign Jews.[10] In October of that year 10,000 Jews residing in Germany but holding Polish papers (the validity of these papers was in some doubt) were summarily expelled from the Reich.[11] Because of the doubtful legal status of these expellees this action was not thought likely to cause much reaction in foreign capitals and it did not.

But this brutal expulsion so disturbed a young Jew living in Paris whose parents were among the expelled, that he shot a secretary of the German legation. This act led directly to the famous pogrom of November 1938, in which for the first time violence was directed against *all* Jewish property and whose perpetrators made no attempt to distinguish between foreign Jews and German Jews. Kristallnacht led to numerous protests from all the democratic states and the German government bowed to this pressure at least to the extent of exempting foreign Jews from paying the fines levied on the German Jewish community.

Under cover of the war the line between foreign and German Jews quickly faded. The Foreign Office official directly responsible for the "Jewish Question," Legationsrat Eberhard von Thadden, described his task as giving "complete protection against complaints and interventions of foreign states in the question of measures taken against Jews."[12] As the process of the "Entjudung" (elimination of Jews) of Germany proceeded apace in 1942 the Foreign Office sought and gained the acquiescence of Germany's allies and friendly states to let the German regime handle their Jewish nationals as the Nazis saw fit. In the case of neutral Switzerland, however, a repatriation agreement was negotiated.[13] Jews who were citizens of enemy states, of course, presented no problem to the Germans.

By 1943 Germany was nearing the state of being "Judenrein" (Jewish free), at least officially. (In fact, many thousands of Jews slipped through the nets in one way or another.)[14] Himmler had given orders that no Jews were to be held in concentration camps in Germany because even that violated the concept of a Jewish-free Germany.[15] In February 1943, however, Himmler reversed this policy to the extent that he authorized the temporary incarceration of a few Jews to be used for "exchange purposes" in Germany. Three criteria were employed for selecting Jews who might be candidates for exchange: first, those with important connections in foreign countries; second, Jews whose fate was of enough concern to outsiders that they could be used to put political and/or economic pressure on the Allies; and finally, prominent figures in public service. These Jews would be offered in exchange for German nationals interned in enemy countries. Himmler's order read: "The Reichsführer-SS intends to establish in Germany a camp for about 10,000 Jews who are French, Dutch, or Belgian citizens, and who on account of their foreign connections could be used to apply pressure to the Allies. Perhaps they could be exchanged for Germans abroad."[16] Individual concentration camp commanders were ordered to draw up lists of candidates for "Austauschjuden" (exchange Jews). In order to house the Austauschjuden, Himmler took over half of a partly empty prisoner of war camp at Bergen-Belsen.[17] This was a permanent camp with reasonably well-built permanent structures.

Here in July 1943 the first transports of Austauschjuden began to arrive. There were four categories of Jews in the first arrivals: first, Greek Jews from Salonika who held Spanish passports; second, the so-called Amerika-Juden, who held South American passports (while some of these Jews were actually South Americans, others had purchased the papers); third, Palestinian Jews, that is those who held valid entry permits to Palestine; and finally, 305 Jews selected from the inmates at Theresienstadt. In all, about 1,500 exchange Jews were moved into the camp in mid-1943. In addition, the camp housed 500–600 men who had been used to prepare the camp for its new inmates. For the first six months after the camp was opened there was little evidence that the exchange scheme would bear any immediate fruit. For the Jews time was largely spent waiting.

In the first half of 1944 the population of the camp more than tripled (from 2,000 to 7,000) and its character also began to change from that of an "Aufenthaltslager," that is, a camp designed to hold prisoners for fairly short periods of time, to a more conventional concentration camp. The principal source of new prisoners was the Dutch camp at Westerbork.[18] Normally, these Jews would have been sent to Auschwitz, but the rapid advance of the Russian armies combined with the growing strain in the German transportation system made it more convenient to use Bergen-Belsen as at least a temporary stopping point. With the arrival of more and more inmates who were not in the Austausch category, the camp became ever more sub-divided into almost hermetically sealed sub-camps, each containing a different sort of prisoner. First, there was the Sternlager, so called because the inmates wore the Star of David on their prison garb. At the beginning of 1944, the Sternlager contained 379 inmates; by the middle of the year this number had risen to 4,000. That number remained more or less constant as deaths, transfers and arrivals approximately balanced each other. These Jews were for the most part "Austauschjuden" and as such were privileged (Vorzugsjuden). Despite that designation, they were forced to endure roll calls up to five hours a day; they performed labor, mostly sorting of clothes and effects of Jews exterminated in the East; and they were subjected to the routine brutality of the guards. On the other hand, the camp officials allowed a committee of inmates to exercise some control over the internal affairs of the camp, and the rations for the Sternlager inmates were rather better than those of ordinary concentration camp inmates. They also had somewhat better medical care—death rates in the Sternlager were quite low throughout 1944. Obviously, if these Jews were to be used for exchange, it was in the interests of the Germans to keep them in reasonably good health.[19]

Across the Hauptappellplatz (principal roll call area) from the Sternlager was the Neutralenlager (camp for neutrals) also known as the Schneebaumlager, after an Argentinian named Joseph Scheenbaum who was the inmate in charge of the Lager (Lageralteste). Here were 200 Spanish, Portuguese and Argentinian Jews. They were not obliged to do any work other than policing their own barracks, and their food and medical care was better than any other inmates in the camp. Also the Draconian punishments inflicted on the inmates in the Sternlager were seldom if ever used in the Neutralenlager.

The third camp within the camp was the Sonderlager which held 350 Polish Jews who held foreign, that is non-Polish, passports. In theory, they were in the same category as the inmates in the Sternlager except that they were from Eastern Europe. Why they were segregated is not known, but there is reason to think that the Germans did not want those men who had seen genocide firsthand to reveal the awful truth to the Western Jews in the Sternlager.

The fourth camp was the Ungarnlager which housed 1,683 Hungarian Jews. Though they wore the Star of David, they did not work and did not have to endure the regimen of roll calls. These Hungarians had arrived on July 8, 1944, specially selected as possible candidates for ransom.

Finally, there was the Häftlingslager with about 1,000 "regular" inmates. Their status was no different from inmates in any other camp.

Life for the Jews in Bergen-Belsen in 1944 was harsh, but rather less so than that of inmates in other camps and the death rates in Bergen-Belsen were less than in any other camp. The prisoners were sustained by the hope that at any moment they might be exchanged. Although no such exchanges were ever negotiated, some 2,000 prisoners were sent to neutral countries and safety. In August and again in December, sizable contingents of Hungarians were sent to Switzerland in return for ransom money.[20] A transport of 310 Amerika-Juden was dispatched to Switzerland as well. About one-half of these arrived, the other half were unaccountably turned back. And finally 222 Palestinian Jews after many adventures finally reached Palestine. Had a disinterested observer visited Bergen-Belsen even as late as the autumn of 1944, he probably would have described it as a very harsh prison, but hardly the "living hell" it was to become in the next months.

The Descent Into The Abyss

The final horror at Bergen-Belsen was the result of two minor, and at the time seemingly unimportant, decisions. The first was to use some of the unoccupied space in the camp as "Erholungslager" (recovery camp) where sick and/or exhausted prisoners could recuperate;[21] and the second, to house Eastern laborers temporarily at Bergen-Belsen. It is difficult, if not impossible, to comprehend the minds of the men who thought up the idea of making Belsen a "rest camp." Did they cynically intend to continue extermination in another fashion after the gassing centers in the East had been overrun? And did they, with their well-known inclination to pervert language, select this innocuous term to cover their evil plan? Or, in that morally inverted world they inhabited, did they really think of the camp as a rest and recuperation center? The German armament industry did have an almost insatiable need for workers, and with the loss of much of the East to the advancing Russians the greatest pool of available manpower (and womanpower) had been lost. That being the case, the policy of squandering the lives of the slave laborers in a prodigal fashion made less and less sense to a rational man. If indeed this was the case—that Bergen-Belsen was really seen as a rehabilitation center, and that view cannot be rejected out of hand—the camp officials never made the slightest effort to realize that goal. The sick were dumped into wholly inadequate facilities and once there received no medical care at all, so that rather than recovering most died. Not once did any inmate really recover sufficiently to be sent back to the arms factories.

On March 24, 1944, 1,000 slave laborers, most of them tubercular, arrived at Bergen-Belsen from the underground factory Dora, where the V-weapons were produced.[22] Working conditions at Dora, a satellite camp of Buchenwald, were extremely harsh. The workers spent most of their life underground in fetid caves working under brutal overseers. In the first half of 1944, of a work force of 28,000, 3,000 died and 3,000 more were "used up" and sent to Auschwitz for extermination. The arrival of the 1,000 sick from Dora created a housing problem for the camp officals. It was decided to house these sick and dying men in the Häftlingslager which sometime in the past had been cleared of its former inhabitants. Without medicine, proper food, or adequate sanitation facilities, infectious diseases were soon at epidemic levels in the Häftlingslager, but since each unit of Belsen was rigidly sealed off from every other unit, the epidemic in the Häftlingslager had little effect on the rest of the camp. From time to time new shipments of sick prisoners arrived who were "dumped" into the Häftlingslager, now referred to as the Erholungslager. By the end of the year there were 1,823 sick and dying prisoners crowded together into barracks which were considered seriously over-crowded when they held half as many.

On August 18, 1944, the SS reported that the total concentration camp population was 524,286. In addition, there were 612,000 men and women, who, though not in camps, were under SS jurisdiction. This number included 400,000 Poles from the Warsaw area; 60,000 Jews from Lodz; and 90,000 Jews from Hungary. None of these were scheduled for immediate extermination; all were seen as potential munitions workers. In the end many were in fact exterminated, but the SS was beginning to waver in its absolute commitment to extermination of all Jews in view of the growing shortage of labor. Many more of the 612,000 would die in transport to the West and others from mistreatment and disease. But many did in fact reach the munitions factories. In August 1944, the SS used an open field adjacent to the Sternlager as a transit camp for Polish women from Warsaw on their way to factories. This camp was called a Durchgangslager (transit camp).

Later it became the infamous first of the two women's camps at Bergen-Belsen. Tents were set up in which the women stayed for a few days or weeks at most. In general, the inmates in the Sternlager reported that the Polish women seemed to be reasonably healthy, not badly dressed (although some did not have shoes) and quite well fed.

As the weather was mild, sleeping under canvas was not a severe trial. Then later in August, new shipments of women began to arrive who were not relatively healthy Poles, but Jewish women from Auschwitz-Birkenau. Himmler had ordered the camp population in the East to be reduced against the day when the Russian advance would resume and the camps would be in danger of falling to the enemy. In October and November, two more shipments of Jewish women from the East arrived.[23]

As the weather turned wet and cold, conditions in the women's camp rapidly deteriorated. Sanitary facilities were almost non-existent and disease took a terrible toll. During the night of November 7, 1944, a storm wrecked the tent city and the women were left at the mercy of the elements. The next day the camp authorities ordered the women's camp abandoned and the women moved into some of the barracks of the Sternlager. The displaced inmates were shifted into several barracks which had been erected some weeks before from the labor camp at Plascow. These barracks had been dismantled and shipped to Bergen-Belsen where they were re-assembled on the Appellplatz (roll call area).

On December 1, 1944, there were 15,257 inmates in Bergen-Belsen, almost all Jews. They were housed in a camp designed to hold only half as many. Conditions in the camp were beginning to deteriorate rapidly. To restore some measure of order, Himmler sent Josef Kramer,[24] commandant of Auschwitz-Birkenau, to Bergen-Belsen. Kramer had the reputation of being a tough, hard administrator, which was what Himmler thought Belsen needed. In a briefing given to Kramer before he actually took command of the camp, he was told, apparently in all seriousness, that as a matter of policy when slave laborers in munition factories missed two weeks of work due to sickness or exhaustion, they were sent to Bergen-Belsen to recover.[25] Once their health improved, they were to be sent back to their factories. It was acknowledged that this scheme was not working out too well and he was exhorted to take the situation firmly in hand. (This briefing seems to come straight out of Kafka. To a normal person it is simply inexplicable. One almost automatically asks, who is kidding whom? But this use of a patina of reason over a vast and murky pool of insane irrationality was quite characteristic of National Socialism.)

Kramer arrived at his new post in early December and moved decisively to straighten the camp out.[26] First, he announced that henceforth Bergen-Belsen would be a proper concentration camp, that is to say all privileges were abolished (n.b. the most privileged of the prisoners, the Hungarians and Amerika-Juden, had already left). Second, Kramer ordered four barracks emptied at once in order to make room for the flood of sick inmates who were constantly arriving. This order, of course, put even more pressure on the already severely crowded situation in the camp. Third, Kramer abolished all vestiges of prisoner government and the Kapo system (i.e., use of "trustees" to preserve order within the camp) was introduced. And finally, a day of fasting for all Jews in the camp was decreed. It is hardly necessary to say that these measures, far from preventing the descent to chaos, actually accelerated it.

In the three months from December 1, 1944, to March 1, 1945, conditions in Bergen-Belsen deteriorated catastrophically. On the former date, the camp held 15,257 prisoners, about double its capacity. On the latter date, the number had grown to 41,520. Since perhaps as many as 15,000 prisoners had died in that three-month period the total influx was between 40,000 and 50,000. Where did they come from? The women, and Bergen-Belsen was fast becoming a women's camp, came from Auschwitz, Gross-Rosen and other Nebenlagern in Silesia that had been emptied in the face of the Russian winter offensive. Some of the women had travelled for as long as six weeks, partly on foot and partly in open box cars. It was not uncommon for the dead to outnumber the living when the sorrowful trains finally reached their destination. And what awaited them at Bergen-Belsen? To accommodate the vast influx of new prisoners, Himmler had acquired the other half of the prisoner-of-war camp which became known as the Grossesfrauenlager. Overcrowding, insufficient food, brutality of the guards and infectious disease took a frightening toll on the survivors. The men shipped to Bergen-Belsen were for the most part used-up workers from the munitions factories.

Genocide took many forms in National Socialist Germany: the execution squads of the Einsatzkommandos, the gas chambers, and the death marches of the winter of 1944–1945. What happened in Bergen-Belsen in the last weeks before liberation was another form of genocide—genocide by cynical neglect and administrative indifference. The figures tell their own story.[27] The death rates in 1943 were very low as one would expect in a camp containing "privileged prisoners" who had a value to the Germans as long as they were alive and well enough to be exchanged.

Number of Prisoners Who Died in Bergen-Belsen in 1943

June	July	Aug.	Sept.	Oct.	Nov.	Dec.	Total
4	2	7	4	7	10	9	47

In 1944, with the arrival of more and more sick and exhausted prisoners, the numbers rose dramatically but remained well below the level of most other camps.

Number of Prisoners Who Died in Bergen-Belsen in 1944

Jan.	8		July	127
Feb.	10		August	93
March	32		Sept.	126
April	390		Oct.	171
May	217		Nov.	338
June	186		Dec.	350
		TOTAL 2,048		

Of the 2,048 inmates who died in 1944 in Bergen-Belsen, 307 were from the Sternlager and the other privileged camps; the remaining 1,700 were from the Häftlingslager. By the beginning of 1945 the recording system broke down (and some of the records were destroyed) so, for the most part, one must use estimates. In January about 1,000 inmates died; in February that number rose to perhaps as many as 7,000. And it must be recalled that thousands more died on the way to Belsen. We do have the figures for March and they reveal more than could any words. In an area about 600×400 yards, 41,000 starving, utterly demoralized and dying prisoners were confined, many without even the most primitive sanitary facilities; the water supply was polluted; food was running out. And into the inferno close to 25,000 (almost 1,000 per day) new prisoners—the majority of them near death—were dumped.

Bergen-Belsen Mortality Figures for March 1945[28]

	HL I*	HL II	FL	UL	SL	Other Camps	Total Deaths	Inmate Population
March								
1.	72	91	73	1	7	1	245	41,520
2.	98	117	68	3	5	2	293	41,972
3.	99	221	67	3	13	—	403	44,964
4.	99	280	64	3	7	—	453	45,815
5.	90	164	81	5	5	—	345	45,233
6.	86	114	86	5	9	—	300	44,872
7.	100	104	70	4	7	1	286	45,054
8.	93	469	78	4	3	—	647	44,872
9.	87	200	85	3	5	1	381	45,166
10.	84	150	86	4	7	—	331	44,785
11.	105	177	89	6	4	1	382	44,457
12.	98	500	92	4	4	—	698	44,649
13.	88	460	116	5	4	—	673	45,958
14.	89	533	93	4	3	1	723	47,834
15.	68	672	121	7	10	—	878	45,117
16.	75	380	112	3	6	—	576	47,313
17.	101	581	152	3	2	—	839	46,742
18.	94	517	153	6	7	—	777	46,608
19.	80	613	131	6	6	—	836	46,504
20.	74	456	165	3	6	—	704	46,176
21.	78	287	160	4	2	—	531	45,478
22.	85	661	168	7	6	—	927	46,804
23.	86	442	166	3	4	—	701	46,336
24.	75	126	191	4	6	1	403	45,638
25.	74	227	187	2	4	—	494	46,806
26.	69	891	181	6	2	—	1,149	46,816
27.	86	231	189	4	5	—	515	45,732
28.	75	344	170	3	4	—	596	45,266
29.	78	434	177	8	12	—	709	45,097
30.	73	65	184	4	8	—	334	44,394
31.	73	728	225	3	10	—	1,039	44,060
Totals:								
	2,632	11,235	3,980	130	183	8	18,168	45,485 (Average)

*HL = Häftlingslager FL = Frauenlager UL = Ungarnlager SL = Sternlager

Even Kramer became so uneasy by the conditions in the camp that he addressed a long letter to the Head of Department D in the SS Administration Department, SS Gruppenführer Glücks. The letter—dated March 1, 1945, and introduced at Kramer's trial by his defense attorney—is important enough to be quoted in full.[29]

Gruppenführer, it has been my intention for a long time past to seek an interview with you in order to describe the present conditions here. As service conditions make this impossible, I should like to submit a written report on the impossible state of affairs and ask for your support.

You informed me by telegram of 23rd February, 1945, that I was to receive 2,500 female detainees as a first consignment from Ravensbrück. I have assured accommodation for this number. The reception of further consignments is impossible, not only from the point of view of accommodation due to lack of space, but particularly on account of the feeding question. When S.S. Stabsarztführer Lolling inspected the camp at the end of January, it was decided that the camp could not hold more than 35,000 detainees. In the meantime this number has been exceeded by 7,000 and a further 6,200 are at this time on their way. The consequence of this is that all barracks are overcrowded by at least 30%. The detainees cannot lie down to sleep, but must sleep in sitting position on the floor. Three-tier beds or bunks have been repeatedly alloted to the camp in recent time by Amt B III, due to lack of transport connection they have not arrived. If I had sufficient sleeping accommodation at my disposal, then the accommodation of the detainees who have already arrived and of those still to come would appear more possible. In addition to this question, a spotted fever and typhus epidemic has now begun, which increases in extent every day. The daily mortality rate, which was still in the region of 60–70 at the beginning of February, has in the meantime attained a daily average of 250–300 and will further increase in view of the prevailing conditions.

Supply. When I took over the camp, winter supplies for 1,500 [probably 15,000] internees had been allocated; some had been received, but the greater part had not been delivered. This failure was due not only to difficulties of transport but also to the fact that practically nothing is available in this area and all must be brought from outside the area. The supplies which were available here were calculated to last til 20th February; by the greatest economy it has been possible to have still, at the present time, potato supplies for eight days and turnips for six days. Fresh negotiations with the representative of the local peasants' combine with regard to further supplies have been started. The same situation prevails with regard to supply of bread—apart from the supply from Training Area Bergen, we received daily one load from a bread factory in Hanover. For the last four days, there has been no delivery from Hanover owing to interrupted communications, and I shall be compelled, if this state of affairs prevails til the end of the week, to fetch bread by lorry from Hanover. The lorries allotted to the local unit are in no way adequate for this work, and I am compelled to ask for at least three to four lorries and five to six trailers. If I had transport here, then I could send out the trailers into the surrounding area. If the negotiations with the representatives of the local peasants' combine on the subject of supply of potatoes are successful, then I have to allow for fetching these by lorry. The supply question must, without fail, be cleared up in the next few days. I ask you, Gruppenführer, for an allocation of transport. The collection of food will be dealt with from here. Further, I need badly an additional supply of boilers. All boilers belonging to the camp are in use day and night. We shall be in great difficulties if one of these boilers fails. There is a field kitchen here with 30 boilers of 300 litres capacity which were placed at the disposal of the S.S. by the D.A.F. We received a written reply on 3rd January, 1945, to our request of 29th December, 1944, that we be allowed to make temporary use of these boilers but this request was denied. S.S. Sturmführer Burger noted this when he paid a visit here. I do not know what decision was made as a result of the discussions. Possibly under the changed conditions it is possible to gain use of the boilers.

State of Health. The incidence of disease is very high here in proportion to the number of detainees. When you interviewed me on 1 December, 1944, at Oranienburg, you told me that Bergen-Belsen was to serve as a sick camp for all concentration camps in North Germany. The number of sick has greatly increased, particulary on account of the transport of detainees, who have arrived from the East recently—these prisoners have sometimes spent eight to fourteen days in open trucks. An improvement in their condition, and particularly a return of these detainees to work, is under present conditions quite out of question. The sick here gradually pine away til they die of weakness of the heart and general debility. As already stated, the average daily mortality rate is between 250 and 300. One can best gain an idea of the conditions of the incoming transports when I state that on one occasion, out of a transport of 1,900 detainees over 500 arrived dead. The fight against spotted fever is made extremely difficult by the lack of means of disinfection. Due to constant use the hot-air delousing machine is now in bad working order and sometimes fails for several days. At the time of this visit S.S. Stabsarztführer Lolling promised me a 'short-wave delousing machine.' To use this I need a more powerful transformer, which, according to information received from Bauinspektion Nord, Wismarer Strasse, Berlin, has not been delivered. Although I require the apparatus urgently, it is impossible at the present time to send transport to Berlin to collect it. The same situation prevails with the parts for the new crematorium and for roofing materials and cement. In my opinion it should be possible for the Building Department to load all these urgently required items, if not in a flatbed lorry, at any rate in a truck, to dispatch them to this place along with a transport of detainees from Sachsenhausen or Ravensbruck. So far as the Building Department is concerned, the matter is finished when they have stated that the items can be fetched from this or that place. The Departments probably believe that plenty of transport is available here and only waiting for employment. A further item which concerns the Building Department is the sewage installation. It was decided in 1943 that the existing machinery was too small for the number of the detainees. In the period since 1943 several investigations and plans were made, but nothing at all done. Now owing to this delay a catastrophe is taking place for which no one wishes to assume responsibility. It may be possible to initiate measures from your end so that the matter is put in hand.

Gruppenführer, I can assure you that from this end everything will be done to overcome the present crisis. With this letter I merely wanted to point out to you the difficulties which exist here. For my part it is a matter of course that these difficulties must be overcome. I am now asking you for your assistance as far as it lies in your power. In addition to the above-mentioned points I need here, above all, beds, blankets, eating utensils—all for about 20,000 internees.

On the question of putting the internees to work, I have contacted the employment authorities. There is a chance of being able to make use of male labor. In addition to the concentration camp prisoners, there are here still about 7,500 internees ('Exchange Jews'). S.S. Haupsturmführer Moes from RSHA. IV. A. 4b. was here last week and informed me that these Jews would be removed in the near future. It would be much appreciated if this could be done as soon as possible, for in this way accommodation could then be found for at least 10,000 concentration camp prisoners. Because of the spotted fever danger S.S. Haupsturmführer Moes is not willing to take these Jews away at the present time. These Jews are to go partly to Theresienstadt and partly to a new camp in Württemberg. The removal of these internees is particularly urgent because several concentration camp Jews have discovered their relatives among the camp internees—some their parents, some their brothers and sisters. Also for purely political reasons—I mention in this connection the high death figure in this camp at present—it is essential that these Jews disappear from here as soon as possible.

With that I wish to close my present report. In this connection, Gruppenführer, I want to assure you once again that I will definitely do everything to bridge over this difficult situation. I know that you have even greater difficulties to overcome and appreciate that you must send to this camp all internees

46

discharged from that area; on the other hand, I implore your help in overcoming this situation.

Heil Hitler, yours truly,

J.K., S. S. Hauptsturmführer

While hundreds of inmates were dying every day in Bergen-Belsen, just two miles away, at the Panzer Training School, 800 tons of food were stored and a bakery capable of producing 60,000 loaves per day was available. Kramer received only 10,000 loaves a week from the Panzer Training School bakery; the remainder he obtained from civilian sources. When these sources were cut off, Kramer did not even bother to request additional food from the army.[30]

The Last Days Before Liberation

Despite Kramer's report, the transports continued to roll into Bergen-Belsen. Even as late as April, two more large transports arrived. The last 15,000 arrivals were housed in a temporary camp at the Panzer Training School some two miles from the Belsen main camp. Reitlinger speculates that the fact that transports continued to pour into Belsen was the work of Eichmann. "The last leering gesture of a man who was going to 'leap into his grave, laughing because he had five million deaths on his conscience.'"[31] Himmler, who by the spring of 1945 was deeply involved in various negotiations with the Red Cross and the neutrals to save what could be saved in the growing turmoil of the camps,[32] appointed S.S. Standartenführer Kurt Becher as "Reichssonderkommissar" for all matters relating to Jews and political prisoners. The actual charge, dated April 4, 1945, read: "In view of the critical sanitary and accommodation situation, I appoint you Reichssonderkommissar for all Concentration Camps."

On the afternoon of April 10, 1945, Becher arrived at Bergen-Belsen to confer with Kramer, who painted a grim picture. There were, he said, 1,000 seriously ill inmates in the camp at that moment (the figure seems much too small); further, there had been no bread deliveries for two weeks; and there was only an eight-day supply of turnips and potatoes. Kramer put the number of deaths per day at between 500 and 600. Dr. Rudolf Kastner, a prominent Hungarian Jew who had accompanied Becher, suggested that the only way to avert a total catastrophe at Belsen was to hand the camp over intact to the advancing British. Kramer agreed. Without having inspected the camp itself, Becher left the same evening for Hamburg where he reported his recommendations (by phone) to Himmler who agreed. On April 11,

47

1945, Becher returned to Belsen carrying the authorization for capitulation. Kastner, who was still with Becher, saw the camp for the first time on the second trip. He later wrote of the experience: "The prisoners in their prison garb sit by the thousands on the ground outside their barracks. They are only living skeletons. We did not see the bodies of the crematorium, but we did see a food storage magazine which was full of Red Cross packages."

Whether Becher ordered the local Wehrmacht commander to parley with the British or whether the military men acted on their own initiative is unclear, but it is a minor point. On April 12, 1945, a Colonel Schmidt, his aide Lieutenant Bohnekamp, a medical officer, and a translator set off to the West in an automobile prominently displaying a white flag. They were met by a British patrol which escorted the Germans to the headquarters of the Eighth British Armoured Corps. Here they met with Colonel Taylor-Balfour who agreed to take over the camp if the Germans in turn would neutralize a square 10 kilometers on each side around the camp. As Schmidt had no authority to conclude such a deal, Balfour agreed to accompany the Germans to their headquarters. There after several hours of parleying the British accepted a somewhat smaller neutralized zone (6 × 8 kilometers). German troops in the area were to help maintain order for a few days and then they were to be allowed to proceed to their own lines. The SS guard was to leave before the British arrived but 80 or so administrative troops were to remain. The actual agreement reads as follows:

> Agreement with regard to Belsen Concentration Camp made by Chief of Staff, I Parachute Army, Military Kommandant, Bergen, and B.G.S., 8 Corps. (1) On instructions from Reichsführer S.S. the Military Commander at Bergen approached the Allied Forces, 12th April, with regard to the concentration camp at Belsen. (2) The following area will be regarded as neutral. [There follow a number of map references.] (3) Both British and German troops will make every effort to avoid battle in this area, and, as far as operations make it humanly possible, no artillery or other fire (including bombing and strafing) will be directed into this area. Equally, neither side will use this area for the deployment of troops or weapons. This paragraph is subject to overriding military necessity. (4) The German military authorities will erect notices and white flags at all the road entrances to this area, so far as possible. These notices will bear, in English and German, on one side 'Danger-Typhus,' and on the other 'End of Typhus Area.' A disarmed post will be mounted by the Germans at each notice-board. (5) Hungarian and German troops at present employed on guard duties will remain armed at their posts. All such troops will wear a white armband on their left sleeves. (6) The Hungarians will remain indefinitely, and will be placed at the disposal of the British Forces, for such duties as may be required. The German

Wehrmacht personnel will be released within not more than six days and conveyed back to the German lines with their arms and equipment and vehicles at the end of the period. (7) S.S. Guard personnel will be removed by 1,200 hours, 13th April, any remaining will be treated as Prisoners of War. S.S. Administrative personnel will (if the Wehrmacht can prevent them running away) remain at their posts and carry on with their duties (cooking, supplies, etc.) and will hand over records. When their services can be dispensed with, their disposal is left, by the Wehrmacht, to the British authorities. (8) The Wehrmacht will continue to man the telephone exchange until it can be relieved. Wires leading out of the camp will require disconnecting.[33]

Liberation

In accordance with the terms of the agreement Kramer ordered the SS Guards to leave Belsen by noon on April 13, 1945. He remained behind with 80 SS administrative personnel, a number of Hungarian soldiers and some miscellaneous German army regulars who were now entrusted with guarding the camp. On that day and the next the British forces in the vicinity of Belsen were heavily engaged in forcing a crossing of the Aller River in the vicinity of Winsen and Walle, and that action delayed for 48 hours the actual liberation of the camp. On the afternoon of April 15th, strong armored units of the British army were on the move down the road leading to the camp. The Commander of the 63rd Anti-Tank Regiment, Colonel Taylor, was named temporary commander of Belsen after liberation.

Taylor ordered a junior officer, Derrick Sington, and two NCOs (between them they knew five European languages) to proceed into the camp with a loudspeaker mounted on a jeep ahead of the lead tanks to advise the inmates that though they were liberated, no one would be permitted to leave the camp for the time being because of the danger of spreading typhus. Both the British and the Germans feared the consequences of 60,000 highly infectious inmates bursting out of the camp and spreading into the countryside. Sington was also told to tell the inmates that temporarily Hungarian troops would remain on duty as guards under British command and that these guards would be under orders to act to prevent anyone from leaving camp. Finally, Sington was to bring the glad tidings that food and medical help was being rushed to the camp with all possible speed. When Sington reached the neutral zone perimeter, he was met by a sign reading "Danger—Typhus" and two lance corporals, one Hungarian and one German. The German soldier handed him a note which read: "Allied Commander, do pay attention!" Sington guessed correctly that this was meant as an invitation to proceed to the camp to meet the German authorities. Sington proceeded to the gate of the SS camp (as opposed to the prison gate) where he was met by Kramer, neatly turned out in a fresh uniform. Sington told Kramer of his intention to make an announcement to the prisoners. Kramer recommended against it saying that "They're calm now. It would be unwise to risk a tumult." Sington thereupon waited for the arrival of Colonel Taylor who ordered Sington to proceed into the camp. With Kramer on the running board as his guide Sington drove slowly through the main gate. Belsen was liberated. His description of what happened next is worth quoting in full.[34]

> I had tried to visualize the interior of the concentration camp, but I had not imagined it like this. Nor had I imagined the strange simian throng, who crowded to the barbed wire fences, surrounding the compounds, with their shaven heads and their obscene striped penitentiary suits, which were so dehumanizing.
>
> We had experienced gratitude and welcome in France, Belgium and Holland. We had been surrounded in Paris, embraced and thanked. In a Flemish village our truck had been loaded with tomatoes and ripe pears, and jugs of cool beer had been handed to us by joyful people.
>
> But the half-credulous cheers of these almost lost men, of these clowns in their terrible motley, who had once been Polish officers, land-workers in the Ukraine, Budapest doctors, and students in France, impelled a stronger emotion, and I had to fight back my tears.
>
> One man standing in the gateway to a compound wore a normal blue suit and smiled a greeting. While our loud-speakers were calling out the announcement, I went and shook hands with him.
>
> "I am Dutchman," he said, "I used to work for the *Nieuwe Rotterdamsche Courant.*"
>
> He was tall and red-haired. He had fought in the International Brigade and was, we discovered afterwards, one of the great figures of the German concentration camps.
>
> As we rolled on through the camp, crowds of prisoners began to surge through the barbed wire into the throughfare. Kramer leaned towards me:
>
> "Now the tumult is beginning," he said.
>
> Suddenly a German soldier began firing his rifle into the air. Gradually he lowered the muzzle until it was firing only just over the heads of the prisoners. I ran across to him and covered him with my revolver.
>
> "Stop shooting," I said.
>
> He stopped firing. But suddenly a dozen striped figures jumped into the crowd hitting again and again with sticks and packing-case strips.
>
> No leaps in a ballet could have astonished me as did the kangaroo jumps. They were like prancing zebras, these creatures in broad-striped garments, careening here and there, smiting to

left and to right, bending double with the impetus of the blows they struck. Or was it a cattle-drive, this onrush of scores of creatures running the gauntlet of fearful blows? And why did they not strike back, defend themselves, instead of dodging, surging on or falling down?

Half-way across the road I saw a thin creature on his back trying to ward off blow after blow from a thick stick.

I tried to understand what I saw. Could these 'policemen' be the political prisoners suppressing criminals among the inmates by the only possible means?

I did not know then that they were hut-leaders 'keeping order' for the SS, nor that the stampeding mob was making for the kitchen beyond the highway. I did not yet understand that mortal starvation conditioned all happenings in the camp.

Passing the big kitchen we came out through a second wire gate opposite the smaller of the two women's camps. Crowds of women, all in the hideous penitentiary garb, lined the roadside. One of them called out in French:

"You must deliver us. It is FRIGHTFUL, this camp."

I went to her, and she said: "We are 400 Frenchwomen here—all political prisoners. You MUST deliver us."

We turned and came up the main throughfare. The men were still cheering, and one wraith-like figure, with a crutch, threw it down and fell on his knees as our car passed, clasping his hands in thanksgiving. We turned left through a barbed wire gateway, entered the larger women's camp, halted and began our announcement.

In a few seconds the car was surrounded by hundreds of women. They cried and wailed hysterically, uncontrolledly, and no word from the loudspeakers could be heard. The compounds of the camp were planted with young birch-trees, and the women plucked leafy springs and small branches and hurled them on to the car. One branch fell on Kramer's shoulder. He brushed it impatiently away.

We drove back to the main entrance. Kramer jumped off the running board and I said to him:

"You've made a fine hell here."

"It has become one of the last few days," he replied.

Half a mile up the road we saw the first concrete buildings of the Panzer Training School. A dozen or so of these formed an overflow concentration camp, housing 15,000 men who had been brought from the Dora Camp near Nordhausen, five days before. Kramer had turned them away, and the German Army commandant had accommodated them, together with their SS gaolers, in these buildings.

Our announcement here was again drowned by the cheering, and we left immediately for the Wehrmacht Kommandantur.

Ceremony and an attempt at an 'official front' were being

51

staged at the Kommandantur. Colonel Harries, commander of the Wehrmacht battalion left behind to help guard the concentration camp, and Colonel Schmidt, whom I had seen in the farmyard at Schwarmstadt three days before, were talking to Colonel Taylor. The two German colonels were dapper and immaculate, and very conscious of their role as trustees of the 'Belsen truce.' Soon after I joined them a British medical officer came in.

"There have been some casualties down at the concentration camp."

Immediately afterwards the telephone rang. A German captain answered it, and then turned to us and said:

"It appears that a loud-speaker went into the camp and that it has started a disturbance."

Colonel Taylor said to Colonel Schmidt: "Who is causing casualties in the camp? Under the agreement only SS administrative personnel may be in the camp and they should be unarmed."

"They may have pistols," said Colonel Schmidt with a shrug of his shoulders.

Colonel Taylor ordered the German colonels to go down with us immediately to the camp.

Kramer came up and saluted as we alighted from our cars at the gate.

"Tell him that all SS must hand in their arms within half-an-hour," said Colonel Taylor to me.

I did so.

"Without arms I can't be responsible for the camp," answered Kramer.

After making this announcement, both at Bergen-Belsen and the overflow camp at the Panzer Training School, Sington, Colonel Taylor, and the medical officer of the Second British Army (Brigadier Glyn Hughes) re-entered the main camp. They were surrounded by a cheering throng shouting everything from "How are you?" to "God Save the King." Later in the day shots were heard as the guards fired directly at prisoners to prevent "plundering," that is, digging potatoes without authorization. Up to that moment, Kramer had acted as if he were on terms of perfect equality with the British, offering them advice, giving suggestions, and in every way deporting himself as a professional helping other professionals in a unpleasant but necessary task. Sington happened to be near Kramer when one of the prisoners went down, shot by a guard. Furiously he turned to Kramer and shouted: "Pick that man up and take him to the hospital!" Kramer looked at Sington with amazement, but when Sington pulled his revolver he reluctantly obeyed. A small incident but a telling one. Sington commented:

It was a strange commentary on their utter ignorance of all Western standards and codes of morals and behavior, that they should have believed their collaboration would be accepted. It also indicates the extent to which their sense of wickedness had been dulled by years of brutish crime. Kramer was revealed afterwards as the man of the "selection" at Auschwitz. Here he had stood before the crematorium as the truck-loads of human cattle were unloaded, motioning frail young women and their children towards the gas chamber, and robuster men able to work, into the Camp. His nostrils must have been unaccustomed to anything except the stench of death.

But his grotesque attempt at collaboration was perhaps indicative of something else. Had the racial teaching of Himmler's schools really succeeded in making these SS men regard Jews and 'Häftlinge' as species of poisonous rat? Did they really feel no more concern at the shooting through the stomach of a beautiful Jewish girl, or the death from slow starvation of an innocent man, than a normal person might feel at the infliction of a similar fate on a rat? It is possible.[35]

After Liberation

During the night of April 15–16, 1945, the stronger prisoners, for the most part new arrivals, looted the food and clothing storerooms of the camp; 50 pigs were slaughtered and cooked over open fires that night by Poles and Russians; and a number of Kapos were killed and some other old scores settled. The British troops fired aimlessly over the heads of prisoners but took no serious action to stop the disorders. Considering everything, the problems of that night (and there was little trouble thereafter) were of a remarkably mild nature.

The next day the British took stock. The camp measured 650 × 400 yards and contained about 80 permanent barracks. Each of these housed between 400 and 800 inmates. There were 40,000 prisoners in the main camp and another 15,000 in the temporary camp at the Panzer Training School. Of those in the main camp, about two-thirds were women (25,000) and, on balance, their condition was worse than that of the male prisoners. Of the women, 18,000 were Jewesses from Hungary, Poland, Romania, Czechoslovakia and Germany. Most of them had come from Auschwitz-Birkenau. In many cases they were the sole survivors of their families. The remaining women were either refractories (conscript workers who had disobeyed the rules and been sent to the camp as punishment) or political prisoners (often meaning partisans or those accused of aiding partisans). The 15,000 male prisoners were also divided between Jews, refractories and political prisoners. The percentage of Jews was lower among the males because several thousand inmates of the Sternlager had been transferred out of the camp shortly before liberation. A large number of the inmates were in a state of almost total demoralization. One wrote a diary shortly before liberation: "There are no more roll calls. Also no work parties. The only thing left to do is to die." Another noted: "A great exhaustion is getting the upper hand. Will salvation come in time?"

The British moved with dispatch to bring some measure of order to the nightmare of Belsen. Food was bought up; a hospital was established at the Panzer Training School; the water supply was improved; and the dead (13,000 unburied corpses littered the camp grounds on April 15th) were buried as rapidly as possible. On April 17, 1945, Kramer was arrested and the SS staff put to work gathering up the dead and taking them to great mass graves scooped out of the ground by bulldozers. On April 24, 1945, Colonel Spottiswoode, who was in charge of directing the medical side of the camp, ordered a number of local civilians to the camp. He had them stand on the edge of one of the mass graves and there addressed them in the following words:

> While we are showing you round this camp, you must bear two things in mind. First, that we British have been here 10 days. We hope that we have cleared the bulk of dead. We have buried several thousand. We have provided food for the survivors. We have given them new hope. The living conditions which you see here today are not so frightful as those which existed under the Germans. Secondly, you must realize that, according to those wretched victims who experienced other camps, this camp was in some respects one of the better ones. Chiefly because in this camp it was possible in most cases, though not in all, to die fairly quietly from hunger or typhus. In certain other camps, the inmates were done to death and hurled into mass graves, sometimes before they were dead. And these are people from every country, of every religion and race in Europe. The only crime of many of them was their patriotism.
>
> What you will see here is the final and utter condemnation of the Nazi Party. It justifies every measure which the United Nations will take to exterminate that Party. What you will see here is such a disgrace to the German people that their name must be erased from the list of civilized nations.
>
> You who represent the fathers and brothers of German youth see before your eyes a few of the sons and daughters who bear a small part of the direct responsibility for this crime. Only a small part, yet too heavy a burden for the human soul to bear. But who bears the real responsibility? You who have allowed your Führer to carry out his terrible whims. You who have proved incapable of doing anything to check his perverted triumphs. You who had heard about these camps, or had at least a slight conception of what happened in them. You who did not rise up spontaneously to cleanse the name of Germany. You stand here judged through what you will see in this camp. You must expect to atone with toil and sweat for what your children have committed and for what you have failed to prevent. Whatever you may suffer,

it will not be one hundredth part of what these poor people endured in this and other camps. It is your lot to begin the hard task of restoring the name of the German people to the list of civilized nations. But this cannot be done until you have reared a new generation amongst whom it is impossible to find people prepared to commit such crimes; until you have reared a new generation possessing the instinctive goodwill to prevent a repetition of such horrible cruelties.

We will now begin our tour.[36]

Despite all the efforts of the British, they were only able to bring the typhus epidemic under control gradually. By the beginning of May, however, the crisis had passed. No figures exist for the first four days but thereafter the records are reasonably complete.

Month	Day	Died	Evacuated	Total in both Camps
April	19	825	—	60,985
	20	696	—	60,289
	21	400	—	59,889
	22	1,250	—	58,639
	23	1,700	—	56,939
	24	1,200	—	55,739
	25	785	—	54,954
	26	343	—	54,611
	27	496	—	54,115
	28	421	—	53,694
	29	326	—	53,368
	30	600	—	52,768
May	1	410	—	52,358
	2	449	4,177	47,732
	3	373	733	46,626
	4	317	98	46,211
	5	209	9,559	36,443[37]

In June the old camp was burned before an audience of 300 former inmates and the British garrison at Belsen. A British officer addressed the assembled troops and former inmates with a speech in which he tried to make some sense out of Bergen-Belsen:

In a few minutes, we are going to burn down the last remaining hut in what was once Belsen concentration camp. I cannot help feeling—the same thought has probably occurred to you too— that in the razing to the ground by fire of this pestilence-ridden camp there is a great symbol. It is, I feel, a symbol of the final destruction for all time of the bestial, inhuman creed of Nazi Germany; the creed by which criminals tried to debase the peoples of Europe to serve their own devilish ends. The British flag has never stood for cruelty and bestiality. That is why it has never yet flown over Belsen Camp. It will fly in a few moments. There too is a symbol; the symbol for the completion of the great task of liberation for which the Allied Nations have striven for six long years, the completion of the task begun by the British Liberation Army when it landed on the beaches of Normandy on June 6th, last year, and the completion, in particular, of the grim but inspiring task with which units of the 2nd Army were confronted here a short while ago.

What has been achieved in that short time? About 40,000 people were still alive when you came here. In addition 10,000 or more lay dead and unburied. You evacuated 29,000 from here, and have had to bury 13,000 who have died after your arrival. You have prepared and staffed the four hospitals and the new transit camps for the final 27,000 survivors. 500 started home four days ago. Another 7,000 began to go home today. This is the achievement of you officers, men and women of the devoted units of the Royal Army Medical Corps; of those magnificent officers and the men of the Royal Artillery; of the Military Government Detachments; of the selfless British Red Cross Detachments and the medical students; of the Swiss Red Cross; and of the Headquarters and Services who have maintained us here.

This moment is the end of a chapter, the pages of which are filled with the vilest story of cruelty, hate and bestiality ever written by a nation. You have closed one chapter in the life of some 27,000 final survivors of this camp. Before this ceremony begins, I would like to pay one special tribute to the British soldier. His great heart, his patience, his sympathy and his sense of humor have always made him the finest ambassador that any nation could wish for.

And now I am going to call upon four of you who have borne the heat and burden of the day since the beginning: Colonels Johnston, Spottiswoode and Mather, and Major Miles, to touch this hut off.

And let's give a cheer as it goes up.[38]

1. Virtually all magazines and newspapers carried some Bergen-Belsen pictures. The most impressive were in the *Illustrated London News* and *Life.*
2. *Spectator,* April 20, 1945.
3. *Times,* June, 1945.
4. Malcolm Proudfoot estimated that there were 660,000 prisoners in the camps at the end of the war and 10 percent of these were Jews. That would put the number of Jewish survivors at between 60,000 and 70,000. In addition, of course, there were about one million (outside the Soviet Union) who survived either because the Germans lost the war before they could complete the Final Solution, or because they somehow avoided the SS dragnets.

Country	Jewish Population 1939	Survivors 1946
Austria	65,000	18,000
Baltic States	250,000	20,000
Belgium	90,000	25,000
Bulgaria	50,000	45,000
Czechoslovakia	315,000	60,000
Denmark	8,500	5,500
France	320,000	160,000
Germany	221,000	22,000
Greece	75,000	10,000
Hungary	400,000	220,000
Italy	50,000	30,000
Netherlands	140,000	36,000
Norway	2,000	750
Poland	3,351,000	80,000
Rumania	850,000	420,000
Yugoslavia	75,000	11,000

Livia Rothkirchen in an article entitled "The Final Solution in its Last Stages" (*Yad Vashem Studies* VIII) says that in her opinion the number of survivors was "even higher" than Proudfoot's estimate. Yehuda Bauer in an article in the same issue of *Yad Vashem Studies* writes: "It would appear that the number of Jewish survivors who remained alive after the epidemic and vicissitudes of the first post-liberation weeks had taken their toll was 100,000 not 75,000 as given by Michael Proudfoot, *European Refugees,* p. 306."

The total number of Jewish survivors at Bergen-Belsen cannot be established with complete accuracy. Feig speaks of 40,000 but offers no evidence for the figure. We do have two fairly solid figures. There were 17,000 Jewish women in the camp on liberation day. We also know that three transports, each containing about 2,500 inmates, left the camp from April 6 to April 9, 1945. On April 6, 1945, 2,500 inmates from the Sternlager, the Ungarnslager and the Sonderlager left. They were eventually liberated by the Americans. On April 7, 1945, a second train carrying Hungarian Jews left. They were eventually liberated by the Russians. On April 9 a third train also carrying 2,500 prisoners left; its fate is unknown except that a few days later in an air raid 56 were killed and 250 wounded. I have found no estimate of the number of Jewish males in the camp on April 15, but 15,000 does not seem an unreasonable figure. To summarize:

Jews in Bergen-Belsen in April 1945

Males in the camp	15,000 estimate
Females	17,000
Evacuated April 6–9	7,500
Total	39,500

Using Proudfoot's figures of 60–70,000 survivors, Bergen-Belsen contained well over half of all the camp survivors. Using Bauer's figures, Bergen-Belsen contained 40 percent.

5. Lucy Dawidowicz, "Belsen Remembered," *Commentary*, March 1968, p. 84.
6. Eberhard Kolb, *Bergen-Belsen* (Hannover, 1962) p. 14. The figures are from S. Adler-Rudel, *Ostjuden in Deutschland 1880 bis 1940* (Tübingen, 1959).
7. A. Graml, "Die Behandlung von Juden fremder Staatsgehörigkeit in Deutschland," in *Gutachten des Instituts fur Zeitgeschichte* (Munchen, 1958). Cited in Kolb, p. 15.
8. Even Goering admitted that "such Jews who really were and who remained foreign citizens, naturally are to be treated in accordance with the treaties which we have with those states."
9. *Voelkisher Beobachter*, March 30, 1933.
10. Kolb, p. 15.
11. "The Polish government fearing that they might well be faced with the dumping of 60,000 Jews of professed Polish nationality . . . passed a decree invalidating the passports of Jews who lived outside Poland unless endorsed with a special stamp which could only be procured in Poland itself . . . Those who failed to do this by October 29th became stateless." On October 28, 1938, 15,000 Jews due to become stateless at midnight were sent up to the Polish border. They were turned back by the Polish authorities. A few days later the Germans "dumped" 10,000 stateless Jews on the frontier near Zbaszyn. Reitlinger, *The Final Solution*, pp. 10–11.
12. Quoted in Kolb, p. 20.
13. *Ibid.*, pp. 22–26.
14. When the war ended there were still almost 8,000 Jews in Berlin.
15. Kolb, p. 34.
16. Quoted in Kolb, p. 33. When the exchange idea was first considered there was some talk of using Eastern Jews. A Foreign Office official in Riga warned his superiors that this wouldn't do. "Since it is known that many thousands of the local and German Jews have been shot in the course of time in the area of Riga, it is questionable whether any Jews can be considered for the purpose of exchanging them without the executions being used against us abroad." Reitlinger, p. 363.
17. The camp was originally to be called "Civilian Intern Camp, Bergen-Belsen" but the name was changed to "Aufenthaltslager Bergen-Belsen" because in accordance with the provisions of the Geneva Convention a Civilian Intern Camp was subject to international inspection. See Kolb, pp. 208–209.
18. On January 11, 1944, 1,037 Jews from Westerbok arrived at Belsen. Included in this transport were diamond workers, men decorated with the German Iron Cross and their families, and half-Jews who belonged to the Dutch Confessional Church. Some of these were later shipped to Auschwitz in October 1944. On February 1, 1944, 773 more arrived; another 210 in March; 101 in April; 238 in May and 178 in July. Between July and the

end of the year about 1,000 male Jews from the Netherlands came to Belsen.

19. The best information on camp life is to be found in the diaries of the inmates. Two in particular are to be noted. Loden Vogel, *Dagboel uit een Kamp* (Den Haag, 1946); and Abel Herzberg, *Tweestromenland* (Arnhem, 1950). Fairly large selections from both, translated into German, are to be found in Kolb's *Bergen-Belsen*.

20. On August 21, 1944, a transport of 318 Hungarian Jews was sent to Switzerland. On December 8, 1944, a second transport containing 1,308 inmates left Belsen for Switzerland. A ransom of 5 million Swiss francs was paid for these lives. See Eugen Levai, *The Black Book of the Martyrdom of Hungarian Jewry* (Zurich, 1948).

21. There is no documentary evidence about this decision. WVHA (SS-Wirtschaftverhaltungshauptamt) directed by SS-Obergruppenfuehrer Pohl had the responsibility of exploiting concentration camp labor. Amtsgruppe D (Chef für Amtsgruppe SS Gruppenfuehrer Gluecks) had direct responsibility for the camps. When Belsen was first established as an exchange camp the WVHA had no authority over it. Only after it was decided to make it into an Erholungslager did it come, in some measure, under the authority of WVHA.

22. See Dr. G. L. Frejafon, *Bergen-Belsen* (Paris, 1947). This is the account by a French doctor of conditions in the Häftlingslager from August 1944 on.

23. In the two months from mid-October to mid-December, six transports of workers (Jewish women) were sent to industrial works.

		Destination
October 19, 1944	750 Polish Jews	Elsnig/Elbe
October 23	300 Hungarian Jews	Markkleeberg/Leipzig
November 11	750 Hungarian Jews	Duderstadt
December 2	300 Hungarian and Polish Jews	Magdeburg
December 6	300 Hungarian Jews	Markkleeberg
December 22	65 Hungarian Jews	Leppstadt

In the same Autumn 8,000 inmates arrived at the camp. In August and September 3,200 workers came from the satellite camps around Buchenwald. On October 18, 1944, a transport of 2,000 women came from Auschwitz-Birkenau; on November 4, 1944, another 3,000 arrived.

24. Kramer replaced a man named Haas. Although the situation in the camp was cited as the official reason for his dismissal, in fact, the real reason seemed to be that Haas had had his portrait painted by a Jewish inmate. When this fact reached Pohl (the head of WVHA) he was full of indignation, calling the act "so unworthy that words fail me . . ." Kramer was born in Munich in 1906; joined the party in 1931; the SS in 1932. In 1934 he was made a guard at Dachau and from that time on was almost continuously employed in one camp or another. His last post prior to Bergen-Belsen was commandant of Auschwitz.

25. "The Trial of Josef Kramer and 44 Others." *The Belsen Trial* ed., Raymond Phillips (London, 1949) p. 160.

26. Kolb, p. 124.

27. *Ibid.*, p. 309.

28. *Ibid.*, p. 312.

29. *Belsen Trial,* p. 163–166.
30. *Ibid.,* p. 178.
31. Reitlinger, p. 506.
32. See *Kersten Memoirs* for the best account of these negotiations.
33. Kolb, pp. 226–227.
34. Derrick Sington, *Belsen Uncovered* (London, 1946) pp. 16–19.
35. *Ibid.,* p. 35.
36. *Ibid.,* pp. 88–90.
37. Kolb, p. 312.
38. Sington, pp. 149–151.

DACHAU

Introduction

The liberation of Dachau, as such, played no role whatsoever in the grand strategy of the Allies. In early 1945 Eisenhower told Marshall that "from the very beginning, extending back before D-Day, my plan has been to . . . make one great thrust to the eastward,"[1] in other words bypass Bavaria and therefore Dachau. On March 28, 1945, however, Eisenhower informed Stalin that in addition to the main thrust toward Dresden, he also planned a secondary advance "to effect a junction with your forces in the area Regensburg-Linz, thereby preventing the consolidation of German resistance in the Redoubt in Southern Germany."[2] This diversion to the South was carried out by General Jacob Devers' Sixth Army Group which consisted of the French First Army (General de Lattre de Tassigny) and the American Seventh Army (General Alexander Patch). By April 25, 1945, the Seventh Army was strung out on an east-west axis just south of the Danube, poised for an advance to the southern frontier of Germany.[3]

On the morning of April 28th the battalion commanders of the 180th regiment of the 45th Division, one of six Divisions making up the Seventh Army, were told by their commanding officer that on the next day "the notorious concentration camp at Dachau will be in your zone of action."[4] The camp was to be seized, but nothing was to be disturbed because "International Commissioners will move in to investigate conditions when the fighting ceases." Shortly after noon on April 29, elements of the 45th Division moved into the town of Dachau itself. The streets were deserted and there was no resistance. Advance patrols pushed on toward the camp itself. On a spur off the Munich rail line these patrols discovered a train made up of 39 coal cars all filled with bodies in an advanced state of decomposition.[5] The train had arrived two days before from Buchenwald. Most of the inmates were apparently dead on arrival, but the few survivors who struggled off the trains were either shot or clubbed to death. Even battle-hardened veterans, to whom death in its ugliest forms was commonplace, were sickened by the sight. The officers quickly took command of the situation and ordered a careful search of the train for survivors and a count of the victims. Stories vary. Some say there were no survivors; some that one man was found alive; some speak of a number of survivors. In all 2,310 bodies were counted.

As the search through the train for survivors was being made, other units of the 45th Division approached the main gate of the camp itself. They were greeted by machine-gun fire from the guard towers, which they answered. At one point the German gunners turned their guns on the Appellplatz, which was rapidly filling with excited inmates. The towers were rushed and all or nearly all the guards were killed. At the same time the Rainbow Division was also advancing on Dachau. At 13:00 on April 29, 1945, the Second Battalion of the 222nd Infantry reached the town of Dachau. An advance party commanded by Brigadier General Linden proceeded directly to the camp where they were met by a representative of the Geneva Red Cross. A young German lieutenant who had arrived at the camp from the front only two days before formally surrendered the camp to the General. According to the divisional history it was the men of the Rainbow Division, not the 45th Division, who wiped out the last German resistance and entered the camp first. The *New York Times* reporter, an eyewitness, wrote that "dozens of German guards fell under the withering fire," and he added that some of the prisoners grabbed the guns of the dead guards and "exacted full revenge."[6] Near the train and thus some distance from the perimeter of the prison he saw the bodies of 16 guards. While the main gate was being rushed, three jeeps carrying soldiers of the 42nd Division as well as the American correspondent Marguerite Higgins entered the camp from the south. As they reached the Appellplatz prisoners shouted: "Are you American?" Higgins made an affirmative nod which, in her words, "caused pandemonium." "Tattered, emaciated men weeping, yelling and shouting 'Long live America' swept toward the gate in a mob."[7] A prisoner named Piet Maas made minute-by-minute entries in his daybook that day. At the moment the Americans entered he wrote: "1728. First American comes through the entrance. Dachau free!!! Indescribable happiness. Insane howling."[8] Thus at 12 minutes before six on the afternoon of April 29, 1945, the 12-year history of the Dachau concentration camp came to an end. Its existence and that of the rule of Adolf Hitler were almost exactly coterminous.

The Last Days Before Liberation

Dachau had been opened in March 1933.[9] In 1941 it was re-classified as an I-A camp, meaning that it was to hold those unable to work, the elderly, clergy, and various prominent personages.[10] In its 12-year history something over 200,000 prisoners were at one time or another at Dachau and about 30,000 died there. From time to time batches of prisoners—Russian officers, for example—were brought to Dachau for execution, but it was not an extermination camp as such. As the war went on the character of the camp changed drastically. By 1944 it still contained clergymen and prominents, but it also became a dumping ground for prisoners from Eastern camps that had been overrun by the Russians. Originally the camp was designed to hold 5,000 prisoners; after 1942 it never had less than 12,000; at liberation the figure was in excess of 30,000. In addition, 40,000 prisoners were in several auxiliary camps (Nebenlager) working in war industries. In the last months of the war the rations had been cut from 1,000 calories a day to about 600. By April 1945 breakfast for the inmates consisted of one-half liter of ersatz coffee or tea; lunch was a liter of thin soup made from potato peelings or dried vegetables; for dinner the inmates were given 6½ ounces of black bread and ¾ ounce of sausage. Twice a week an ounce of margarine was given out.[11]

This starvation diet left the inmates with virtually no strength to fight off the typhus introduced by the new arrivals from the East. In December 1,800 inmates died; in March 4,000; in April the rate had risen to 200 per day.[12] Into this chaotic nightmare the Germans continued to pour additional prisoners throughout April. On April 26, 1945, a group of 120 women arrived. They were the survivors of a group of 480 who had left Auschwitz in January and had been on the march for much of the preceding three months. The next day, only 48 hours before liberation, 1,600 half-naked men stumbled into the camp, the survivors of 2,500 who had left Buchenwald two weeks before.[13] On the same day 2,300 arrived on the death train referred to in the introduction to this chapter. These figures explain how it was possible that despite the staggering death rates the population of the camp continued to increase almost to the end.

In these last hours one question was uppermost in the minds of all the inmates: Would the Germans kill them before the liberating armies arrived? They had good reason to be alarmed. According to the testimony of Hoess, the commandant of Auschwitz, Himmler had originally ordered the camps given over to the enemy, but Hitler countermanded this order. Hoess explained:

> After Buchenwald had been occupied, it was reported to the Führer that internees had armed themselves and were carrying out plunderings in the town of Weimar. This caused the Führer to give the strictest orders to Himmler that in the future no more camps were to fall into the hands of the enemy, and that no more internees capable of marching would be left behind in any camps.[14]

Himmler's masseur, Kersten, not always the most reliable source, gave a different version of Hitler's motives. He said Hitler ordered the liquidation of all inmates "to insure that they do not emerge as victors after liberation by the allies."[15] Whatever the source and motivation of the liquidation orders they were undoubtedly given. Himmler told his camp commanders:

> Should the situation develop suddenly in such a way that it is impossible to evacuate the prisoners . . . they are to be liquidated and their bodies disposed of as far as possible . . . the liberation of prisoners or Jews by the enemy . . . must be avoided under all circumstance. Nor must they fall into their hands alive.[16]

On April 14, 1945, Himmler specifically told the commandant of Dachau:

> Surrender is out of the question. The camp is to be immediately evacuated. No inmate is to fall into the hands of the enemy. The inmates at Buchenwald have behaved appallingly toward the civilians.[17]

There is some evidence that Kaltenbrunner even ordered the bombing of Dachau by the Luftwaffe. It is true that when confronted with an affidavit at Nuremberg to this effect, Kaltenbrunner adamantly denied ever giving such an order. (He also denied knowing about the existence of Jewish work camps as branches of Dachau.)[18]

As rumors were received at Supreme Allied Headquarters that the Germans were on the point of liquidating all surviving prisoners at Dachau and Mauthausen, Eisenhower ordered plans to be drawn up to drop paratroopers to take and hold the camps until the ground units arrived. These orders were not implemented because of the rapid Allied advance in the last days of April.[19]

On April 23 the Germans began to evacuate the camp. As a first step late that night all Jews in the camp were ordered to report to the Appellplatz. There they stood until morning. In the course of the night 60 of them died.[20] The survivors were then loaded into boxcars which stood on the siding until the 25th awaiting an engine. When the engine finally arrived and the train departed it seemed certain they would all be killed or die of hunger, thirst, or exposure in the train. On April 27 a contingent of 6,700 men was marched out of the camp to the South apparently to help construct defensive works in the Southern

Redoubt.[21] In a secluded area about 15 miles from Munich the guards turned their guns on the prisoners. Only about 60 survived to tell of the massacre.[22] On that same day the so-called prominents were removed from the camp. In their numbers were Kurt Schuschnigg, the last chancellor of Austria; Pastor Niemoeller; Peter Churchill, a cousin of the English Prime Minister; and two British agents, Best and Stevens, who had been captured in November 1939. The prominents were heavily guarded by SS troops and it was clear they were all marked for death, but as it turned out the SS failed to carry out their orders and all survived. The remaining prisoners were convinced that soon the whole camp would be cleared and there was little chance for survival once they left the camp.

The tempo of evacuation, which was steadily increasing after it commenced on the 23rd, came to a halt on the 27th for three reasons. First, the continual arrival of new prisoners caused considerable confusion and put additional strain on the already collapsing German administration. Second, the prisoners increasingly refused to obey orders. For example, a roll call was ordered and only 200 inmates responded. When inmates were ordered to draw rations for the evacuation journey they managed to extend the operation for most of the day when it could easily have been completed in two or three hours. The German guards, fearing typhus, were reluctant to get close to the prisoners and drive them on with whips and dogs. The passive resistance of the inmates was organized by a group of prisoners called the International Committee which had assumed the leadership role in the camp in the last days before liberation.[23] The third reason for the interruption of evacuation had to do with the arrival, on April 27, 1945, of a Swiss representative of the International Red Cross, Victor Maurer, bringing food for the prisoners.[24] The German Commandant would not allow Maurer to inspect the camp, but he did express a desire to have the Red Cross oversee the repatriation of 17,500 inmates. No German, Jewish or Bulgarian prisoners were to be released, however. Nothing came of the offer, but Maurer was allowed to observe the distribution of the food parcels. From the prisoners he learned that 15,000 had died of typhus since the beginning of the year and that the prominents and 6,000 others had left the camp that morning. Maurer's presence almost surely inhibited the German plans, for the latter were increasingly preoccupied with their own personal safety as the rumble of the American guns became ever louder. On the morning of April 29 with the appearance of the Americans imminent, the last SS guards were preparing to leave. Maurer in his report to his superiors gives a vivid description of the last hours before liberation.

> The atmosphere was strange; wherever one looked there were signs that made you think that the troops that had been in the barracks had fled. Furthermore, the roar of battle was closer. Arriving

at the front gate about 10:30 I met the soldiers who were guarding the camp; a white flag now floated from one of the principal
towers. Most of the officers, soldiers and employees had left the
camp during the night. I remained with a German lieutenant until
the camp was delivered to the Americans. He and his soldiers had
intended to abandon the camp containing 35–40,000 prisoners,
and it was only after lengthy negotiations that I persuaded him to
change his mind, but with the following conditions:
    1. Sentries should remain in the towers to keep the prisoners
under control and prevent them from escaping.
    2. The soldiers not on guard to remain in the courtyard,
unarmed.
    3. A guarantee should be made that the remaining members
of the German garrison would be allowed to retreat to their own
battle line.
These conditions were most happily accepted, for otherwise there
would have been a catastrophe; if thousands of prisoners,
motivated by a desire for vengeance had been allowed to escape,
the people in the bordering region would have suffered; it is
impossible to predict the damage that might have resulted from
the epidemic.
    A few hours later most of these guards were killed in the
skirmish with the Americans at the main gate.[25]

The Situation in the Camp Immediately After Liberation

The exact number of inmates in Dachau immediately after liberation
was impossible to determine. Some had left without authorization;
many died in the first hours of freedom. A quick count revealed the
following approximate breakdown by nationalities:

Poles	9,200	Czechs	1,600
Russians	4,200	Germans	1,200
French	4,000	Belgians	900
Yugoslavs	2,900	Dutch	600
Italians	2,200	Hungarians	600

There were in addition smaller numbers of Greeks, Austrians, Croats,
Norwegians, Serbs, Danes, English, and even a few Americans. There
were about 2,700 Jews in camp but they were not counted as a separate
nationality and were included in the totals of the nation of their origin.
At the Allach camp (a Nebenlager) there were about 3,000 more Jews
who had been employed as industrial slaves. It would seem, then, that
there were about 8,000 Jews in the Dachau system (3,000 at Allach;
2,700 in Dachau; and 2,400 who had been evacuated on the 25th). If the
total population of the Dachau system was 70,000 then this figure con-

forms quite closely to the estimate that Jews made up about 10 percent of the inmate population in Germany at the time of liberation.[26] Typhus was epidemic in the camp; all the prisoners suffered from severe malnutrition; sanitary facilities were virtually non-existent; the water supply had broken down; there was no electricity; hundreds of unburied bodies were strewn all over the camp. There were 4,205 patients in the camp hospital, and the death rate exceeded 200 per day. The conditions were "beyond the range of the experience of the medical profession in western Europe."

In late 1944 as the Allied armies crossed the German frontier SHAEF first came face to face with the problem of displaced persons, and it was obvious that the problem would grow enormously as the advance continued into the interior of Germany. To meet the impending crisis SHAEF set up a training school where a number of officers and enlisted men were formed into teams (DP teams) and trained to handle the immediate problems anticipated in the first days after liberation.[27] On April 30, 1945, less than 24 hours after liberation, DP Team 115 arrived at Dachau. It was commanded by Lieutenant Charles Rosenbloom and consisted of a doctor, a supply officer, an adjutant and six enlisted men. Their mandate was clear; save as many lives as possible. All supplies were to be drawn from local sources and any resistance from the German civilians was to be met with the reminder that "we come as conquerors."[28]

Rosenbloom took a 20-minute tour of Dachau soon after his arrival and commented: "A lot to do." The team set to work at once to bring some measure of order to the camp and to save all who could be saved. The first order of priority was to bring the typhus epidemic under control and provide adequate hospital care for the sick. To accomplish this medical supplies, beds, more doctors, orderlies and above all DDT were needed. The urgent requests from Rosenbloom were passed straight up through the chain of command to Eisenhower himself who ordered all units under his command to give full and immediate assistance.[29] On May 1, 1945, the 116th Evacuation Hospital arrived commanded by Colonel Lawrence C. Ball and began at once converting the former SS barracks into a hospital. In short order, the 116th was joined by the 10th and the 66th Field Hospitals as well as the 1st Medical Laboratory and elements of the 59th Evacuation Hospital. Soon afterwards the United States Army Typhus Commission, commanded by Colonel John Snyder, was on the scene. This unit had prevented a typhus epidemic from breaking out in Naples in 1943, and had ample experience in controlling the disease. Seventy-two hours after the first American troops entered the gates of the camp a full-scale DDT dusting program was underway which quickly brought the incipient epidemic under control. In short order electrical service was restored; water mains repaired, elementary sanitary facilities organized, and a general clean-up instituted. Much of this work was done by the inmates themselves.

Given the magnitude of the crisis the army reversed its original policy of forcing the Germans to provide provisions for the inmates. On May 1, 1945, a convoy of army trucks arrived at Dachau carrying 24 tons of corned beef, 13 tons of rye soup, 15 tons of beets and potatoes, 23 tons of biscuits, as well as large amounts of sugar, marmalade, sausage, evaporated milk, coffee (ersatz), soap and other supplies. With the arrival of ample quantities of foodstuffs the doctors were faced with the paradoxical problems of trying to prevent near starving patients from over-eating.

The problem of the disposal of bodies was given high priority by the DP team on the day they arrived. Some were buried in nearby sand pits; others were cremated at the rate of 200 per day, but these measures were insufficient. The American military command therefore ordered the mayor of Dachau to supply work parties to carry out the task. Carts were filled with bodies and taken to a nearby hilltop where bulldozers had scraped out deep pits. Inmates dressed in their blue-striped uniforms acted as pallbearers. Three army chaplains administered a graveside service. An American corporal who witnessed the burial wrote the following lines entitled *Dachau, Germany*.[30]

> Through quiet Dachau's cobbled streets
> The bull-drawn carts plod their way,
> Past shops, cafes, and cool retreats,
> Past churches where the townfolk pray.
> On through the town they haul their freight
> Of starved and naked dead—
> Up to the hill where the mass graves wait—
> At last the end of fear and dread.

On Saturday, May 5, 1945, Jewish services were held in the camp. A former Albanian Minister of Propaganda named Ali Kuci who was one of the leaders of the International Committee, made the opening remarks. He said that all inmates were aware of the exceptional intensity of the suffering endured by the Jews under the Third Reich. "Along with all free men I rejoice that the Jews of Dachau are at last able to resume their religious life without hinderance." After Kuci's remarks, an American army rabbi named Eichorn delivered the following:

> My Jewish Brethren of Dachau:
> In the portion we read yesterday in our holy Torah we found these words: "Proclaim freedom throughout the world to all the inhabitants, hereof; a day of celebration shall this be for you, a day when every man shall return to his family, and to his rightful place in society."
>
> In the United States of America, in the city of Philadelphia, upon the exact spot where 169 years ago a group of brave Ameri-

cans met and decided to fight for American independence, there stands a marker upon which is written these very same words: "Proclaim freedom throughout the world to all the inhabitants thereof." From the beginning of their existence as a liberty-loving and independent people, the citizens of America understood that not until all the peoples of the world were free would they be truly free, that not until tyranny and oppression had been erased from the hearts of all men and all nations would there be lasting peace and happiness for themselves. Thus it has been that, throughout our entire history, whenever and wherever men have been enslaved, Americans have fought to set them free; whenever and wherever dictators have endeavored to destroy democracy and justice and truth, Americans have not rested content until these despots have been overthrown.

Today I come to you in a dual capacity—as a soldier in the American Army and as a representative of the Jewish community of America. As an American soldier, I say to you that we are proud, very proud, to be here, to know that we have had a share in the destruction of the most cruel tyranny of all time. As an American soldier, I say to you that we are proud, very proud, to be your comrades-in-arms, to greet you and salute you as the bravest of the brave. We know your tragedy. We know your sorrows. We know that upon you was centered the venomous hatred of power-crazed madmen, that your annihilation was decreed and planned systematically and ruthlessly. We know too that you refused to be destroyed, that you fought back with every weapon at your command, that you fought with your bodies, your minds, and your spirit. Your faith and our faith in God and in humanity have been sustained. Our enemies lie prostrate before us. The way of life which together we have defended still lives, and it will live so that all men everywhere may have freedom and happiness and peace.

I speak to you also as a Jew, as a rabbi in Israel, as a teacher of that religious philosophy which is dearer to all of us than life itself. What message of comfort and strength can I bring to you from your fellow Jews? What can I say that will compare in depth or in intensity to that which you have suffered and overcome? Full well do I know and humbly do I confess the emptiness of mere words in this hour of mingled sadness and joy. Words will not bring back the dead to life nor right the wrongs of the past ten years. This is no time for words, you will say, and rightfully so. This is a time for deeds, deeds of justice, deeds of love . . . Justice will be done. We have seen with our own eyes and we have heard with our own ears and we shall not forget. As long as there are Jews in the world "Dachau" will be a term of horror and shame. Those who have labored here for their evil master will be hunted down and destroyed as systematically and as ruthlessly as they sought your destruction . . . And there will be deeds of love. It is the recognized duty of all religious people to bestir themselves immediately to assist you to regain your health, comfort, and some measure of happiness as speedily as possible. This must be done. This can be done. This will be done. You are not and you will not be forgotten men, my brothers. In every country where the lamps of religion and decency and kindness still burn, Jews and non-Jews alike will expend as much time and energy and money as is needful to make good the pledge which is written in our holy Torah and inscribed on that marker in Philadelphia, the City of Brotherly Love.

We know that abstractions embodied in proclamations and celebrations must be followed by more concrete, more helpful, fulfillments. We do not intend to brush aside the second part of the Divine promise. Every man who has been oppressed must and will be restored to his family and to his rightful place in society. This is a promise and a pledge which I bring you from your American comrades-in-arms and your Jewish brethren across the seas:

You shall go out with joy, and be led forth in peace.
The mountains and the hills shall break forth before you in
    singing;
And all the trees of the field shall clap their hands.
Instead of the thorn shall come up the cypress,
And instead of brambles myrtles shall spring forth;
And God's name will be glorified;
This will be remembered forever.
This will not be forgotten. Amen.[31]

The service ended with the choir of Hungarian girls singing "God Bless America." The American film director George Stevens filmed the proceedings for the Army Signal Corps.[32]

After Liberation

The policy of the Western Allies *vis-à-vis* displaced persons, an omnibus term used by SHAEF which included the so-called "slave laborers" as well as the inmates of concentration camps, was perfectly straight-forward.[33] The Allies intended to handle the massive problem in two not very distinct stages. First, immediately after liberation all possible aid would be given to the victims with the object of saving as many lives as possible and restoring the sick to health. This preliminary stage, it was hoped, would last no more than a few days or at most a few weeks and would blend naturally into the second stage: repatriation. As soon as the DPs were physically able to return to their homes they were encouraged to do so. All repatriation, however, was to be voluntary—no one was to be forced to return. The only exception to this rule was in the case of Soviet citizens who, in accordance with Stalin's demands, were to be returned to the Soviet Union whether they desired to be or not.[34]

70

The first stage was reasonably successful, and within a few weeks infectious diseases had been brought under control and the sick were being nursed back to health. As expected, most DPs were anxious to return to their homes as soon as possible, and even before VE-Day the roads of Germany were crowded with former slave laborers and concentration camp inmates making their way back to their homelands. In all something over 11 million people were classed as DPs requiring repatriation. By the end of August, 1945, 500,000 French citizens had returned home; 298,000 Belgians; 326,000 Dutch; 800,000 Italians; 2 million Soviet nationals; 1,593,000 Poles; 367,000 Czechs; 200,000 Yugoslavs—in all 9.8 million.

Who was left? First, the overwhelming majority of those still in the camps in the autumn of 1945 (about 1.5 million) were Poles, Hungarians, Bulgarians, Rumanians, Balts, and Soviet nationals who had refused repatriation.[35] There were also a small number whose health did not permit travel. Most of the central and east European Jews also remained in the camps. Their position was anomalous. Since they were not considered a separate national group, they were scheduled to return to their countries of origin. However, in many cases that country no longer existed (the Baltic states, those portions of Poland which had been incorporated into the Soviet Union, for example). Furthermore some who had returned to their homelands—Poles for example—were met by violence and sometimes death.[36] Given this situation the American authorities were not inclined to encourage repatriation, but neither could they offer any alternative. As a result the former inmates were left in temporary camps awaiting a decision on their fate.[37]

In this discouraging situation, two leaders emerged who organized the Jewish DPs in southern Germany and gave the community—such as it was—a sense of direction. The first to emerge was an American rabbi, Dr. Abraham Y. Klausener, who had arrived in Dachau in the third week of May.[38] First, he acquired an automobile to travel from camp to camp in Bavaria in order to compile lists of survivors. He simultaneously wrote letters to various organizations in the United States describing the conditions in the camps and soliciting help. And lastly, he induced the American occupation authorities to remove the Jewish survivors from Dachau to more acceptable quarters.

But Klausener recognized that in the long run the only way to provide for the needs of the Jewish DPs was to organize them and then convince the American authorities that the Jews had a right to be recognized as a separate national group. In July UNRAA gave Klausener office space in the Deutsches Museum in Munich, and there he established a kind of informal office to offer advice and counsel to individuals and groups while at the same time negotiating with the American occupation authorities. The idea of organizing the surviving Jews into a national community received powerful stimulation when on June

20, 1945, units of the Palestinian Jewish Brigade arrived in Bavaria. They bought relief supplies which were sorely needed and hope which was in greater demand. "As crowds surged around the soldiers and clung to them, a current of mutual discovery and sympathy was generated. For these emissaries, unlike the Allied liberators, had come to seek out their families and their people, to instill courage and hope, to organize and lead an exodus to the land of Israel."[39]

The work of Klausener was to some extent paralleled by that of Zalman Grinberg, a Lithuanian, a doctor and a former inmate of Dachau.[40] He was one of hundreds of Jewish inmates who had been taken by train from Dachau on April 25, 1945. Two days later near the village of Schwabenhausen the train came to a halt; the SS guards warned the prisoners to stay where they were and then disappeared. Led by Grinberg, the prisoners walked to Schwabenhausen and demanded that the mayor provide them with food, shelter, and aid for the sick and wounded. The mayor not only refused their request, he ordered them back to the train. According to his own account Grinberg shouted, "Herr Burgermeister, how would you like to swing from the tree this time tomorrow? The Americans are coming and all crimes will be punished!" The mayor decided that discretion was the better part of valor and rescinded his order. A sympathetic Catholic doctor suggested that Grinberg transport his sick and wounded to a nearby German army hospital which formerly had been a monastary of St. Ottilien. Ambulances were procured and while the transfer was underway the Americans arrived. So enraged were the soldiers at seeing the conditions of the former inmates that they ordered a number of German civilians to line up against the wall with an apparent intention of shooting them. Only Grinberg's intercession dissuaded the Americans from carrying out their intention.

St. Ottilien became an informal camp-hospital housing about 600 former inmates. When the German doctors at St. Ottilien objected to Grinberg's take-over, an American major, Otto B. Raymond, took charge. He managed to get extra ambulances fom the American authorities and also ordered the arrest of the local Nazis.[41]

Grinberg's gratitude to the Americans in general and those who helped him in particular was characteristic of virtually all the inmates in the first days after liberation. The attitude of the Americans—their righteous indignation, their stern administration of justice—was also characteristic. By mid-summer, however, this enormous reservoir of mutual goodwill had begun to evaporate. The Jewish DPs grew impatient sitting day after day in the camps while their former comrades had long since returned home.

On July 1, 1945, at a camp in the German town of Feldafing, 43 delegates representing the various camps scattered over Bavaria met to formulate a policy for the future.[42] The final act of the assembly was a resolution addressed to the leaders of the Allied powers then about to meet at Potsdam asking that all Jews who wished to emigrate to Palestine be permitted to do so as a first step toward creating a Jewish state in Palestine.[43]

While there is no evidence that any of the Allied leaders read the Feldafing Manifesto, that document represents—in a sense—the end of the story of liberation and the beginning of the diplomatic, political, and military history that led to the founding of the state of Israel. The spirit of the liberation was captured perfectly by a poet, who had been an inmate of Dachau, when he wrote: "Sixty-one days of April and May were our Genesis. A great chasm opened between past and future; though everything at the moment of liberation seemed strange, a hope seethed within us that the Allied conquerors might be the bearers of the Ark that would deliver us from the Deluge."

By summer a former inmate noted that the Jews in the camps "were liberated but not free." And this was the central paradox of the liberation. As reports of growing unrest of the camps reached the ears of President Truman, he sent a former Commissioner of Immigration and Naturalization, Earl J. Harrison, to Germany "to inquire into the condition and needs of the displaced persons in Germany, who may be stateless or non-repatriable, particularly Jews." Harrison's report perhaps overstated the case, but he did forcefully call the attention of the President and the American people to the inescapable fact that the "liberated" Jews were still living behind barbed wire and guarded by foreign soldiers. "As matters now stand," he wrote, "we appear to be treating the Jews as the Nazis treated them except we do not exterminate them."[44] This statement was unfair to the local military authorities, to be sure, but not completely off the mark.

Truman ordered Eisenhower to do whatever necessary to improve the conditions in the camps. On September 17, 1945 (the Day of Atonement), Eisenhower visited Felfading. He addressed the 5,300 inmates:

> I am especially happy to be in a Jewish camp on the holiest day of your year. For the time being, you are here and you must be patient until the day comes when you can leave for whatever destination is yours.
>
> The United States Army is here to help you. And it must rest with you to maintain good order and friendly relations with the established authorities. I know how much you have suffered and I believe that there is still a bright day ahead of you.

Eisenhower ordered the rations in the camps to be increased from 2,000 to 2,500 calories per day and he also ordered new quarters to be found for about one-half the inmates at Feldafing to relieve the obvious over-crowding, but on the most vital issue of all—the question of the ultimate destination of the Jewish DPs—neither he nor the American government was able to make a firm commitment.

On November 1, 1945, 40 former officials of Dachau went on trial charged with violations of the laws and usages of war. The trial ended in December. Thirty-six of the defendants were sentenced to death by hanging; the others received sentences ranging from 10 years to life.

1. See John Ehrman, *Grand Strategy 1944–August 1945* (London, 1956) p. 121.
2. The Papers of Dwight David Eisenhower: *The War Years,* vol. IV. p. 2551. (Baltimore, 1970). See also Rodney Minott, *The Fortress That Never Was: The Myth of Hitler's Bavarian Stronghold* (New York, 1964).
3. The Seventh Army was composed of three corps—VI, XXI, XV. The XV Corps liberated Dachau. Its order of battle at the time of liberation was as follows:
   42nd Division (Major General Harry J. Collins)
   222nd Infantry Regiment (Lt. Col. Lucien Bolduc)
   232nd Infantry Regiment (Col. Alfred McNamee)
   242nd Infantry Regiment (Lt. Col. George S. Fricke)
   45th Infantry Division (Major General Robert T. Frederick)
   157th Infantry Regiment (Col. Walter P. O'Brien)
   179th Infantry Regiment (Lt. Col. William P. Grace)
   180th Infantry Regiment (Lt. Col. Everett W. Duwall)
4. Michael Selzer, *Deliverance Day: The Last Hours of Dachau* (Philadelphia, 1978) p. 38.
5. There are a number of accounts of the train and they differ somewhat in detail. See, for example, *Time* May 7, 1945; *New York Times,* May 1, 1945; United States Senate, 79th Congress, 1st Session. Report of the Committee requested by General Dwight D. Eisenhower to the Congress of the United States relative to atrocities and other conditions in Concentration Camps. May 15, 1945. Document 47. (Washington, D.C.). The Congressional committee arrived at Dachau only hours after liberation and thus saw the train before it had been cleaned up. "As we visited Dachau we saw on a railroad track paralleling the main highway and close to the gates of the prisoner camp, a train of cars which had been used to bring additional civilian prisoners to this camp. These cars were an assortment of odd boxcars, some of which could be locked, and some were the coal-car type. In each of them the floor of the car was covered with dead emaciated bodies. In some of the cars there was more than enough to cover the floors. In size, the cars were of the small European type, which, when used for the movement of troops, would never accommodate more than 40 men. Nevertheless, the Army officials in charge of the camp advised us that there were 50 of these cars in this one train and that at least 100 of these civilian prisoners had been jammed into each car—locked in—and that they had been on the road for several days without food and water and that approximately 3,000 of them were dead on arrival and that most of the others were in a dying condition." This account differs in some details from that of Selzer which I have used. See Selzer, p. 171.

6. An eyewitness, Nico Rost, recorded the scene in his daybook (*Goethe in Dachau* [Hamburg 1981]) p. 244. "The SS men in the gate building and the watch towers were shot down by the Americans. We heard the shots and saw them fall." The official history of the Seventh Army asserts that the Americans tried to protect the guards from the fury of the inmates and even, at one point, had to fire over the heads of the prisoners to restore order. See Seventh Army. United States Army in France and Germany 1944–1945. Report of Operations. III, pp. 831–832.

7. *New York Herald Tribune*, May 1, 1945.

8. Quoted in Selzer, p. 195.

9. See Martin Brozart, "The Concentration Camps 1933–1945," in *Anatomy of the State*, pp. 428–437 for an authoritative summary.

10. Konnilyn Feig, *Hitler's Death Camps* (New York, 1981) p. 51.

11. Marcus Smith, *The Harrowing Hell of Dachau*, pp. 105–106.

12. The figures are from the daybook of an inmate, Edgar Kupfer-Koberwitz. p. 245. They conform quite well with estimates made by the Americans after liberation. (*Die Mächtigen und die Hilflosen: Als Häftling in Dachau* [Stuttgart, 1957]).

13. *Ibid.*, p. 251. "April 27. A new convey arrived, no one knows where it came from. They say it is 2000 Italians. They must have brought many sick and weak with them."

14. IMT, IX, p. 407.

15. Felix Kersten, *The Kersten Memoirs, 1940–1945* (New York 1956) p. 342.

16. Quoted in Whitney Howe, *Tyranny on Trial* (Dallas, 1958) p. 343.

17. Rost gives the text of the order in an appendix, p. 247.

18. See IMT XI, pp. 283–286 and XXXIII, p. 281.

19. Malcolm Proudfoot, *European Refugees 1939–1952: A Study in Forced Population Movement* (Evanston, 1956) p. 306.

20. Smith, p. 144.

21. Kupfer-Koberwitz, who actually saw this group leave, estimated it to be about 6,000. From an affidavit of a survivor: "Only 60 could escape the transport. The rest were murdered . . . " See Smith, p. 148. Selzer gives the number as 6,881 and says about half of them were Jews. He gives no source for his figures, nor does he say anything about their fate.

22. Among other acts the underground committee burned all the records in the camp labor office and ordered the prisoners to change the identifying triangles which each prisoner wore. Smith, p. 147.

23. The committee was made up of a Frenchman, a Pole, a Russian, and an Englishman named Connolly. See Selzer pp. 101–115 for a description of the activities of the committee just prior to liberation.

24. XII Report of a Representative of the International Red Cross of his activities at Dachau from April 27, to May 2, 1945.

25. Smith, p. 97.

26. See Proudfoot, p. 306. Other authorities peg the figure a bit higher.

27. *Ibid.*, p. 132. See also pp. 147–152 which contain a summary of the basic document called SHAEF Plan of June 4, 1944.

28. Smith, p. 81.

29. *Ibid.*

30. *Ibid.*

31. Selzer, pp. 224–226.

32. See Donald Richie, *George Stevens* (New York, 1970).

33. See Proudfoot, pp. 120–152 for the administrative history of UNRAA and the Displaced Persons Executive (DPX)—these being the two agencies charged with the problems of handling displaced persons.
34. *Ibid.,* pp. 208–210 has the text of the agreement.
35. All figures from *Ibid.,* p. 189 ff.
36. Bauer reports the fate of hundreds of Jews who had been persuaded by a representative of the Polish government to return "home." At the border they were met by a government official who notified them that they had been sentenced to death for collaborating with the enemy. In view of the victory, however, the head of state had consented to commute their sentence and they would accordingly be permitted to expiate their crimes by three years of hard labor or army service. The men were forcibly separated from their families and children, loaded onto trucks and driven away ... Those who managed to get away returned to the camps in order to warn their brethren and prevent them from meeting a similar fate. Bauer, *The Organization of the Holocaust Survivors,* p. 134.
37. On June 20, 1945, the total number of Jewish DPs in the American zone was estimated to be between 19,000 and 29,000. They were principally in six camps.

Dachau	2,190	Munich-Freiman	1,544
Ebensee	1,438	Geretsried	1,800
Feldafing	3,309		

38. Bauer, p. 142 ff.
39. Leo Schwarz, *The Redeemers,* p. 15.
40. *Ibid.,* p. 3 ff.
41. *Ibid.,* p. 7.
42. *Ibid.,* p. 22.
43. *Ibid.,* pp. 22–23.
44. Proudfoot, pp. 326–330.
45. Schwarz, p. 40

BUCHENWALD

Introduction

The liberation of Buchenwald does not figure as prominently in the history of the Holocaust as the liberation of Bergen-Belsen, simply because by the time the Buchenwald liberation was accomplished there were relatively few Jews in the camp. But leaving aside the question of numbers, the liberation of Buchenwald is significant in any study of the Holocaust because it reveals in the starkest possible fashion the inner dynamics of the camps and the relationship between the Jewish prisoners and all others. Jews at Buchenwald were not only the most mistreated of the various prisoner groups by the guards, they were also subjected to mistreatment at the hands of those prisoners who administered the internal affairs of the camp for the SS. Even now, with passions cooled by the passage of time, it remains difficult to strike a fair balance between the accounts of the last days of the camp as given by the communists, the non-communists, the various national groups and by those not associated with any of these groups. Most survivors, however, agreed that some form of collaboration with their keepers was morally justifiable, despite the dangers they perceived in this behavior.

Christopher Burney, an inmate, said of those who collaborated with the Germans,

> ... they abused for their own ends positions which should have been used in the service of their fellow men; in that they brought death and distress to thousands when they could have saved hundreds; and that they forgot the sacred rule, that he who sets himself up as an aristocrat must first learn that *noblesse oblige.*[1]

The Camp

Buchenwald was opened in 1937 as a camp for hardened criminals and soon acquired a reputation as the worst camp in Germany.[2] By the time of the outbreak of war a large number of "political criminals" had been sent to the camp, most but not all of them German communists. In the weeks following Kristallnacht (November 11, 1938), several thousand Jews were sent to Buchenwald for a few weeks and then released. Up to mid-1944 the numbers of Jews in the camp was generally quite small. On October 17, 1942, Himmler ordered those Jews in Buchenwald to be sent East for extermination; the only exception was 200 Jewish stone masons. This order was issued in line with the general policy of creating a *Judenfrei* Germany. In May 1944 the policy of not incarcerating Jews in German camps was reversed due to growing labor shortages in the munitions industries. As a result tens of thousands of Jews were transported to Buchenwald and its 136 Aussenkommandos (auxilliary camps). These Aussenkommandos varied in size from the Boltewerke in Arnstadt, a manufacturer of cylinder blocks which employed approximately 87 slave laborers, to the great underground factories, code-named Dora, which produced jet engines and weapons using 15,000 or more slave laborers.[3] With evacuation of the Eastern camps in January 1945, the population of Buchenwald was increased to over 90,000.[4]

In the first years of its existence the criminal elements in Buchenwald exerted considerable control over the internal workings of the camp, but with the coming of communists in 1939, a power struggle ensued. In the end, the more highly disciplined communists won a clear-cut victory and by 1942 were in complete control.[5] An American report written shortly after liberation stated, "The Communists maintained excellent discipline and received a certain amount of direction from outside the camp. They had brains and technical qualifications for running the various industries established at the camp. They made themselves indispensible."[6] The SS appointed a communist to be "chief trustee" (*Lageraelteste Eins*) who in turn saw to it that his comrades were put in most of the positions of authority, including the labor office (assignment of prisoners to labor details); the food supply office ("While the SS controlled the quantity of food that entered the camp, it was the prisoners who portioned it out," wrote one survivor); and the hospital. The report goes on: "Hospital facilities were largely devoted to caring for members of the Communist Party. All scarce drugs (and many were scarce at Buchenwald) were reserved for communist patients, and hospital food was available for members of the Party even if not absolutely necessary."

In 1944 a second prisoner organization was formed, led by the Englishman Christopher Burney, which spoke for and gave leadership to the non-communist elements in the camp. Both the communists and their rivals had guns and ammunition, and they cooperated to some extent in the face of the common enemy. The prisoner leaders, on the whole, had the easiest jobs to perform and were, on balance, much better fed and cared for than the average prisoners. Most of the Jews were segregated and did not play a role in the deliberations of the camp leaders. In fact, at the critical moment of the evacuation the leaders, communist and non-communist alike, agreed to sacrifice their Jewish comrades rather than risk a premature uprising. One of the best historians of the Holocaust, Gerald Reitlinger, admits that under the circumstances the decision may have been the right one.[7]

The American Advance

In early April 1945, with Model's army completely surrounded in the Ruhr pocket, the three American army groups—the First, the Ninth, and the Third—started forward again. Their goal was a link-up with the Russians and the final destruction of Nazi Germany. Though spectacular advances were made and Germans surrendered in ever larger numbers, many units of the Wehrmacht, even in last days of the war, still fought on tenaciously. On April 6 the 4th Armored Division overran the town of Ohrdruf.

On the outskirts of the town they discovered a cluster of wooden huts which constituted what was left of Ohrdruf-Nord, the first of the Buchenwald Aussenkommandos to be liberated. Just inside the gate lay the bodies of 29 prisoners, all shot in the back of the neck. The execution had taken place a few hours before. The Americans also came upon 52 naked bodies, covered with lime, awaiting transportation to burial pits in the forest. These pits contained between two and three thousand bodies. As late as April 1, 1945, about 1,000 Ohrdruf-Nord prisoners had been digging a tunnel which was to be used for an underground factory. With the approach of the Americans the camp had been evacuated. On the morning of April 6 a small detachment of German soldiers with two busses came to remove the last prisoners, but the Germans, fearing the Americans might arrive at any minute, shot the sick prisoners instead. The only survivors were a dozen or so men who had hidden themselves about the camp and lived to tell the story. The Americans were filled with indignation and a burning zeal to prove to the doubting German civilians that the horrors of the regime were, if anything, even worse than had been imagined. Lieutenant Colonel James van Wagenen, the Fourth Armored's military government officer, ordered the mayor of the town, Albert Schneider, to see firsthand the handiwork of the National Socialist regime. The mayor, a Nazi, was horror-struck. He admitted that he had heard rumors, but he said he could not believe that Germans would be capable of such acts. It was agreed that the next day the mayor would call together 40 prominent citizens to be taken on a tour of Ohrdruf-Nord. That night the mayor and his wife committed suicide, apparently overcome by shock and grief.[8]

On April 7 units of the VII Corps of the First Army entered the Nordhausen Concentration Camp, which like Ohrdruf was an Aussenkommando of Buchenwald. Here the Americans found 3,000 unburied bodies and 2,000 prisoners too weak to have been evacuated.[9]

On April 8 Third Army Headquarters picked up a signal from a radio constructed secretly at Buchenwald. The message ran: "To the Allies. To the Army of General Patton. Concentration Camp Buchenwald calls! S.O.S. We ask for help. They are going to evacuate us. The SS will exterminate us."[10] The Third Army radio operators received the message and filled the airways with the tidings that help was on the way.

Late in the afternoon of April 11 a tank column of the 4th Armored Division racing down a road at 25 miles per hour encountered a strange and wondrous sight: several hundred concentration camp inmates, in tattered rags but well armed, marching eastward. Their officers gravely saluted the passing Americans. The inmates reported that only a short time before the prisoners had driven the SS from the camp and were now in hot pursuit of the enemy. The Americans reasonably ordered the inmates to return to the camp accompanied by two Psychological Division Officers (Lieutenants Edward Tennenbaum and Egon Fleck). When Tennenbaum and Fleck arrived at Buchenwald they found the camp securely in the hands of the inmates with a white flag flying triumphantly from the main watchtower.

The Prisoners' Revolt at Buchenwald

The last weeks in Buchenwald were times of high anxiety for the prisoners. It was widely believed that Himmler would order mass extermination of the remaining prisoners rather than let them fall into the hands of the advancing Americans. Prisoners feared that even if no such order was given, the camp would surely be evacuated, and for many evacuation was equivalent to a death sentence. On April 3, 1945, the Camp Commandant, Hermann Pister, solemnly promised the camp leaders that he would give the camp over to the Americans intact rather than order an evacuation. The prisoners quite rightly saw this as a ruse to cover the real German intentions.

The International Committee of prisoners met in secret session to determine a plan of action. The camp was still guarded by 3,000 heavily armed SS men so it was decided that an uprising would be suicidal. Instead they decided to bide their time and act if, and only if, either a

1. Mauthausen. May 6, 1945. Tanks of the 11th Armored Division entering the Main gate. The banner in the background was made by Spanish Loyalists, some of whom had been in the camp since 1940.

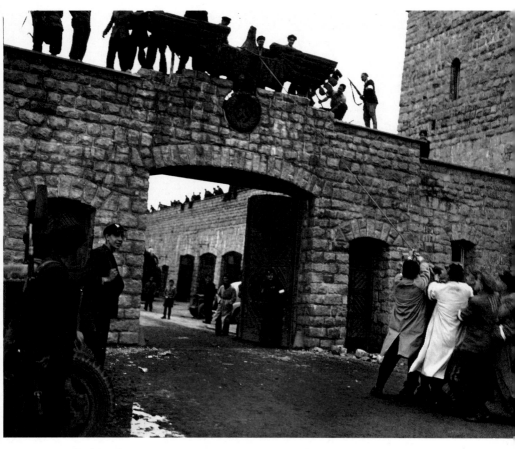

2. Mauthausen. May 6, 1945. Prisoners pulling down the National Socialist
emblem over one of the gates.

3. Mauthausen. May 6, 1945. Prisoners in their barracks, some too weak to stand.

4. Mauthausen. May 6, 1945. Crippled Polish and Russian prisoners photographed in front of an American armored car.

5. Buchenwald. May 1945. American newspaperman Lowell Thomas viewing the bodies of prisoners.

6. Buchenwald. May 1945. Senator Alben Barkley of Kentucky viewing bodies of prisoners being taken to a mass grave.

7. Buchenwald. May 1945. German civilians from Weimar were forced to go through the camp. Here they view the gallows.

8. Buchenwald. May 1945. A fastidious and well-fed German walking through the prisoners' mess hall.

9. Buchenwald. May 1945. Reactions of middle-class Germans from Weimar to the horrors of the concentration camps.

10. Buchenwald. May 1945. Guided tour of the crematorium.

11. Buchenwald. May 1945. The U.S. Army identified this photograph as follows: "Six-year old war orphan with Buchenwald badge on his sleeve waits for his name to be called at roll call at Buchenwald camp, Germany. A United Nations Relief and Rehabilitation Administration worker is calling off names of children in the group of 350 orphans scheduled for departure to Switzerland. The children, who range in age from five to 18 years, are all orphans of the war and some of them have been at the camp for as long as six years. They are Polish, Russian, Yugoslavian and Czech."

12. Buchenwald. May 1945. Jewish children leaving the camp for France.

13. Dachau. May 1945. Dead SS guards, killed in a skirmish with Americans, outside a guard tower.

14. Dachau. May 1945. As American troops of the 7th Army approached the concentration camp, they came upon a train containing the bodies of several thousand prisoners who had died of starvation, exposure or disease. In the picture German youth are being shown the handiwork of the National Socialist regime.

15. Dachau. May 1945. Cpl. Larry Mustinsk of Philadelphia handing out
cigarettes to prisoners.

16. Dachau. June 1945. Polish prisoners paying respect to the American liberators during a national celebration held in the camp.

17. Dachau. May 1945. About thirty minutes after the fighting stopped, German soldiers surrendering to American troops.

18. Dachau. May 1945. Polish prisoners celebrating shortly after liberation.

mass evacuation was ordered or an attempt was made to exterminate the prisoners. The next day all Jews were ordered to the Appellplatz, but for the first time an order of the SS was defied. Only a few showed up; the rest, encouraged by the International Committee, remained in their barracks. The camp leaders explained to the SS that the Jews feared what would happen to them if they obeyed the order. The SS officer, in turn, explained that he only intended to turn them over to the Americans. In the meantime Jews removed the distinctive yellow stars from their prisoner garb to make it more difficult for the SS to identify them. The order was thus frustrated and there was no immediate retaliation, a sure sign that the nerve of the SS was weakening. On April 5 the last Appell was held in which 81,450 inmates were present in Buchenwald and its Aussenkommandos, divided as follows:

35,881	"able-bodied" prisoners in the main camp
2,542	prisoners in hospital
9,330	prisoners being transported from the Aussenkommandos to the main camp
33,704	prisoners in Aussenkommandos

It was estimated that there were about 8,000 Jews among the prisoners, mostly Hungarians and Poles. Daily more and more survivors from the Aussenkommandos were trudging into the camp, putting even greater strain on the already collapsing administration system.

April 6, 1945, was the critical day for Buchenwald. With the Americans still many miles and hours away, orders were given for the arrest of 46 camp leaders and the mass evacuation of the camp on the following day.[11] The communists' intelligence network got wind of the arrest order before it could be carried out and the 46 leaders were warned in good time to go into hiding. The International Committee was not able to stop large-scale evacuations, but they were able to use various stalling tactics to prevent a mass evacuation. From April 7 to 10 more than 25,000 prisoners were taken from camp, few of whom survived until the end of the war. A large percentage of the Jews were evacuated at this time. The communists argued that by sacrificing many they saved some and that any attempt to stop the evacuation by armed force was not only doomed to almost certain failure, but would probably have led to liquidation of the entire population in a camp. The moral issues raised are complex and admit of no easy answers.

On April 11, 1945, there were still 21,100 inmates in Buchenwald. American tanks could be seen on the horizon and the bulk of the SS men had left although the watch towers were still manned. At 2:30 in the afternoon the order was given to storm the watchtowers. The battle lasted only 45 minutes. At 3:15 prisoners unfurled a large white flag from the staff on the main gate, symbolizing victory. Some prisoner units had left the camp in pursuit of the SS, those met by the advancing Americans and ordered back into the camp. At 3:40 the two American lieutenants arrived, but stayed for only a short time. It was not until April 13 that the American army took over the camp. As the first major camp to be liberated Buchenwald was visited repeatedly in the next few days by various delegations. There were so many visitors that, in fact, the American doctors complained that their work was impeded by the necessity of showing VIPs around the camp. At Eisenhower's suggestion, Churchill sent a delegation drawn from members of the House of Commons and the House of Lords, and the U.S. Congress sent a committee as well. Eisenhower and Patton also paid a visit. Eisenhower wrote to Marshall:

> The things I saw beggar description. While touring the camp I encountered three men who had been inmates and by some ruse or another had made their escape. I interviewed them through an interpreter. The visual evidence and verbal testimony of starvation, cruelty and bestiality were so overpowering as to leave me a bit sick. In one room where there were 20–30 naked men killed by starvation, General Patton would not enter. He said he would get sick if he did so.[12]

And in a follow-up letter, also to Marshall, Eisenhower said:

> We continue to uncover German concentration camps for political prisoners in which conditions of indescribable horror prevail. I have visited one myself and I assure you that whatever has been written on them to date has been understatement.

With the arrival of American occupation forces on April 13, 1945, the prisoners were obliged to give up their weapons. The order was obeyed with some reluctance, but finally the communists bowed to *force majeure*. On April 16 the Mayor of Weimar informed his people of the orders of the American commanding officer in the following proclamation.

> The Commanding General yesterday evening ordered that at least 1,000 inhabitants of the city, half of whom are to be women, are to view the camp at Buchenwald and the hospital attached to it in order to be convinced of the conditions at the camp before they are altered. Those who are required to make the trip include: men and women from 18 to 45, particularly those who belonged to the NSDAP. Two-thirds of those are to be of the more prosperous classes and one third the less. They must be strong enough to endure the march and the inspection (it will last about six hours; the distance is 25 kilometers). Food is to be brought and it is to be consumed before viewing the camp. Nothing will happen to the partakers. The march will be accompanied by trucks of the German Red Cross and doctors in order to give help if anyone need it.[13]

In the days before the arrival of the Americans some of the prisoners spread out into the countryside in search of food, but when Hitler was informed of the looting by escaped prisoners he ordered that in the future there were to be no survivors in the camps.[14]

A Jewish survivor named Unsdorfer movingly described the difference between the Jewish inmates and all the others: "The face of every Jewish inmate mirrored a vivid picture of the Jewish people: a crippled and shrunken people, a race that had suffered the most tremendous spiritual as well as physical onslaught in the history of mankind; a race of orphans, widows and widowers . . ."[15] He was saved from total despair by the arrival of an American Jewish chaplain.

> As Chaplain Schechter intoned the Evening Prayer, all the inmates inside and outside the blocks stood in silence, reaccepting the Torah whose people, message, and purpose Hitler's Germany had attempted to destroy. History repeated itself, just as our forefathers who were liberated from Egypt accepted the Law in the desert, so we, the liberated Jews of Buchenwald, reaccepted the same Law in the concentration camps of Germany.[16]

Neither the histories (mostly East German) nor the physical remains of the camp give more than a hint that tens of thousands of Jews died there. To the East Germans, Buchenwald is an important shrine because most of the German communist leaders were imprisoned there. For this reason they have written all of the major histories of the camp, and these accounts repeatedly emphasize the communist role in running the camp, in its liberation and in the post-liberation period. As is customary the communists divided the prisoners into national groups, and since there was no "Jewish Nation" Jews were simply subsumed under the nation of their origin. For example, on May 1, 1945, a giant May Day celebration was held in the camp. The Czech prisoners put on a pantomime, the Yugoslavs sang folk songs, the Poles danced, the Russians did acrobatics, etc., but the Jews are nowhere mentioned. In August the camp was taken over by the Russians, and a few weeks later the last inmates departed. Some time later the East German government made Buchenwald into a major shrine commemorating the camp's communist martyrs. Five memorials were erected at the camp, one of which is dedicated to the Jews who died there.

Though the Jews are largely ignored in the histories of the camp, a few Jewish survivors did carry out an interesting social experiment in the immediate aftermath of liberation. On June 3, 1945, several Jews asked the American officials for permission to form a kibbutz. Permission was granted and a confiscated farm put at their disposal. The point of the experiment was to provide experience for their hoped-for emigration to Israel.[17]

Buchenwald has provided some of the most interesting accounts in the body of concentration camp literature. The Austrian journalist Eugen Kogon survived for seven years in the camp and wrote what is still one of the most terrifying descriptions of life in the camps. Elie Wiesel was at Buchenwald when the war ended and wrote movingly of the experience (see Appendix C). Englishman Christopher Burney was held in Buchenwald in the latter stages of the war and wrote a first-class exposition of the inner workings of the camps. And finally, Walter Bartel, who after the war became the head of the German Institute for Contemporary History, was in Buchenwald for six years. He has written extensively on the camp and edited the most comprehensive account of Buchenwald.

1. Christopher Burney, *The Dungeon Democracy* (New York, 1948) p. 54.
2. Walter Bartel, ed., *Buchenwald: Mahnung und Verpflichtung* (Berlin, East Germany, 1960) pp. 15–96.
3. See Jean Michel, *Dora* (1979) for a personal account.
4. The following table gives a graphic picture of the numbers.

Year	Arrivals	Deaths
1937	2,912	48
1938	20,122	771
1939	9,553	1,231
1940	2,525	1,772
1941	5,890	1,522
1942	14,411	2,898
1943	42,177	3,516
1944	97,866	8,644
1945 (first three months)	43,827	13,056

5. Burney, p. 34. "So in the end the situation stabilized and the Reds . . . held undisputed power with the rifles of the S.S. behind them. How did they use their power? Remember first of all that they were fanatics. Their minds had for many years been poisoned that they and they alone were the elite, that they and they alone had any right of authority over their fellows, and remember that that idea was the only straw which saved them from falling into the abysmal despair of a total inferiority complex. Secondly, that idea had been instructed by the dogma of terror. Who is not with you is against you, and the simplest method of correcting him is to eliminate him . . . an empire had been entrusted to them, a small empire, but one which was nevertheless capable of much wider significance in the course of time. Were they to ignore the chance to help, perhaps even to lead, world revolution from these small beginnings?"
6. Donald Robinson, "Communist Atrocities in Buchenwald" in *The American Mercury* (October, 1946) pp. 397 ff. The author was an official military historian and based the article on intelligence reports. It is not particularly well balanced but the reports do make fascinating reading.
7. Reitlinger, pp. 464–465. "The 'illegal committee' at Buchenwald had arms at their disposal, but not enough to fight 3000 SS guards. They, therefore, decided on a policy of sacrificing the lives they deemed least worthwhile. Mr. Christopher Burney admits candidly that 6000 Jews, demanded by the

SS on April 2 were not thought worth fighting over. Similarly on April 6th when it was a question of making up 8000 people for a transport to Theresienstadt the committee weeded out those—Jews or Gentiles—that they considered 'Cretins'. This is not the sort of thing that happens in adventure books for boys, but it is part of the character of the SS State and Mr. Burney is to be praised for his frankness."

8. Earl Ziemke, *The U.S. Army in the Occupation of Germany* (Washington, D.C. 1975) p. 323.
9. *Ibid.,* pp. 234 ff.
10. Klaus Brobisch, *Widerstand in Buchenwald* (Berlin, East Germany 1977) p. 150.
11. Bartel, pp. 532 ff.
12. Alfred Chandler, ed., *The Papers of Dwight David Eisenhower: The War Years* (Baltimore, 1970) IV, p. 2,623.
13. Bartel, p. 559.
14. IMT, D, p. 749 (Affidavit Hoess).
15. S. B. Undsorfer, "The Yellow Star," in Jacob Glatstein, et al., eds., *Anthology of Holocaust Literature* (New York 1968) p. 261.
16. *Ibid.,* pp. 261–262.
17. Journal of Kibbutz Buchenwald, "Homecoming in Israel," in Leo Schwarz, ed., *Root and Branch* (New York, 1949) p. 315.

MAUTHAUSEN

Introduction

The liberation of each of the camps was at once similar and yet at the same time utterly unique, but one element never changed: the liberators inevitably pronounced their camp "the worst." In some sense, of course, they were all right. Each camp had its own special horrors. The Germans, however, considered Mauthausen to be the harshest of the non-extermination camps and indeed so designated it. To be sent from another camp to Mauthausen was the equivalent of a condemnation to death in its most brutal form. The camp was constructed in 1938 shortly after Austria was annexed. At first it held common criminals and some political offenders who were considered incorrigible. As the war went on the camp expanded and at its high point had nearly 80,000 inmates in the main and 30 or so subsidiary camps. Until 1944 there were only a handful of Jews in Mauthausen, mostly Dutch, who had arrived in three shipments of a few hundred each in 1941 and 1942. Within days of their arrival all were dead.[1] Then in mid-1944 large numbers of Hungarian Jews who were working on defensive lines in the German Alps as well as Jews from the death camps in the East began to pour into Mauthausen. Death rates were staggering. Between January 1, 1945, and liberation on May 8, 1945, 28,080 inmates died and another 3,000 died in the days immediately following the arrival of the Americans.

Liberation

In the first days of May 1945 the Twelfth Corps of the Third Army was advancing in an easterly direction through Bavaria. Some weeks before SHAEF had been awash with rumors that the Germans had constructed a "Southern Redoubt" where fanatical last-ditch resistance could be expected.[2] Eisenhower had shifted units to the South to prevent the Redoubt from forming. By May, however, it was increasingly clear that the Redoubt existed only in Goebbels' fantasy world, and the Americans met only light and sporadic resistance as they advanced through southern Bavaria and into Austria.

In Mauthausen the approach of the Americans led to a growing uncertainty on the part of the camp commandant, Franz Ziereis, as to what he should do with his charges. At one point he received orders to hand over the camp intact to the Americans; shortly thereafter this order was countermanded by Kaltenbrunner and Ziereis was told to increase executions to 1,000 per day. At least this is Ziereis' account of the matter; Kaltenbrunner vehemently denied the allegation at Nuremberg. On April 23 a Red Cross official arrived in an effort to persuade Ziereis to hand the camp over to the Americans. Ziereis refused but he did consent to release 183 French prisoners to the Red Cross. The Red Cross official wrote to his superiors:

> My personal impressions on the subject of the camp are as follows: Something mysterious and terrible seems to hover over all; naturally this impression was somewhat stronger at night . . . on our arrival we were the witnesses of a tragic scene. Five columns of workers each comprising 100 men approximately, entered the camp exhausted after a day of painful work. In each column there were many who were carrying their comrades because their exhaustion could not permit them to continue and they were close to death.[3]

A few days later a second Red Cross convoy entered Mauthausen, bringing packages to the inmates. Ziereis refused to let the Red Cross officials enter the camp to distribute the packages. He finally consented to send a telegram to Kaltenbrunner asking whether this would be permissible. After a three-day wait and no reply the official had a second interview with Ziereis.

> I had talks with Ziereis on the situation in the camp, lack of bread, of clothing, of shoes, terrible lack of linen . . . the sick were five to a bed; in all 60,000 human beings, men, women and children, but Ziereis did not hesitate to execute every morning 30–40 prisoners with a bullet in the neck. The chimney of the crematorium smoked day and night. During these days the prisoners received no bread and sanitary conditions were at the lowest.[4]

On the night of May 2–3, 1945, the official learned that Ziereis had orders to gather all the prisoners in Mauthausen and the Nebenlagern in tunnels at the Gusen camps and blow them up. When the Red Cross official demanded that this order be countermanded Ziereis refused, claiming that he had his orders. Forty thousand prisoners were to be assembled in the tunnels and then blown up with 24 tons of dynamite. The Red Cross official wrote of this interview:

> I found myself alone with Ziereis. All of a sudden in front of me, another man, feeble and trembling, aged and discouraged. He asked me what he could do. He got up and started to play with his pistols. I followed his movements with more curiosity than fear. Suddenly, he said, "Your stay in the camp is not very agreeable for you, I put my house at your disposal; it is outside the camp, away from the scenes which you find upsetting. I have taken the decision to go to the Russian front with a party of troops. That will leave more than 2,000 men to guard the camps and that is sufficient . . ."
> An hour later he conducted me with Reiner to his house. We visited, with terrible calm, the children's room, drawing-room, hunting room with trophies and armaments, all over the house, the farmyard, the beehives, the swimming pool, but I preferred to stay in the camp with the prisoners than in the house of this monster . . .
> There was agitation in the camp; machine guns were reinforced on the guardposts; the stores of hand grenades were distributed here and there; the SS soldiers constructed new machine-gun posts. The defense of the camp was reinforced overall. The camp was in ferment. I was worried.[5]

The Red Cross official, in an effort to prevent the planned murder of the surviving inmates, asked the Burgermeister of the nearest village, St. Georgen, to see that the anti-tank defenses were not manned so that the approaching Americans' arrival would not be delayed. The Burgermeister agreed warmly. Next the official made contact with the American advance guard. He asked for several tanks and several hundred men to disarm the remaining SS, the Volksturm and the Austrian police who together formed the garrison of Mauthausen. He assured the Americans that they would not meet with any resistance and indeed they did not, the villagers greeting them as liberators. By the time they reached the camp itself a white flag was flying.

The initial American impression is well summarized by a colonel who was one of the first to enter the camp.

> At once nauseating and fascinating, these vestiges of Nazi terror made the ordinary American almost doubt what he saw with his own eyes. Harder to doubt was what he smelled with his own nose. The worst discovery of this nature was reserved almost for the last. On 5th May, 1945, a reconnaissance party from TPD 41st

Cavalry Squad 11th Armoured Division advancing down the beautiful valley of the Danube, uncovered in the area two concentration camps, Mauthausen and Gusen. The former was such a spectacle of horror as subsequently to compete in the opinion of the world with Dachau and Buchenwald for the title of worst camp, the worst example of its kind. It was certainly the most hideous thing that many members of the 12th Corps had ever seen. Here were 16,000 political prisoners representing every country in Europe all reduced to living skeletons and ridden with disease. The IND pamphlet of 11th Armored Division reports, "the bodies of more than 500 were stacked in an area between the two barracks. The few longterm prisoners still alive said that at least 45,000 bodies had been burned in the crematories in four years." As one 12th Corps officer wrote home, "It is really the smell that makes a visit to a death camp stark reality. The smell and the stink of the dead and dying, the smell and the stink of the starving. Yes, it is the smell, the odour of the death camp that makes it burn in the nostrils and memory. I will always smell Mauthausen."[6]

On May 8, 1945, the Camp Resistance Committee posted the following notice:

COMRADES

The crimes of Hitler's Nazism are horrible and dreadful. This concentration camp happens to be one of them in which the greatest portion of these atrocities took place.

Many of our comrades were slaughtered as an offer of death to Fascism, many suffered damage to their health of which they can never recover.

The International Court of Investigation of War Criminals has sent its representatives here. It is our duty and our right to assist this work by disclosing these crimes.

Everyone of you who knows anything at all about the following matters should make his name known to his block secretary so he can be called in as a witness. The matters are as follows:

1. Murder of comrades, which you yourself experienced.
2. Shooting while trying to escape, which you yourselves saw.
3. Knowledge of prisoners of war.
4. Sadistic tortures which you experienced and saw yourself.

Report at once because the work must go forward and also so that relations may be notified.

Sgd. A. SOSWINSKI[7]

On May 11, 1945, the first accurate count of the survivors was made. There were on that day in the main camp 15,211 men and 2,079 women. The number of Jewish survivors is not recorded but it probably was not above 10 percent; among them was the celebrated Nazi-hunter, Simon Wiesenthal.

By June 1 virtually all of the French, Belgian and Dutch prisoners had been repatriated leaving only 5,200 survivors still in the camp. On the night of May 13–14 Ziereis, who had been lurking about in the vicinity, was spotted by a prisoner. An American patrol was sent to apprehend him; he opened fire and in the exchange of gunfire was severely wounded. He was taken to 131st U.S. Evacuation Hospital where he was operated on by a former inmate. His wounds proved mortal but he lingered on for several days, during which time he was interrogated by Charles Hager, Agent 511, U.S. Intelligence Service. Ziereis' final statement, rather rambling and not especially accurate, is reproduced at the end of this chapter.

Mauthausen was the last camp to be liberated by the Western powers, and as the liberation came on the same day as the surrender of Germany it was little noticed in the press. By May the horror stories of the camps had become more or less routine. For that reason Mauthausen has never become a symbol in the same sense that Auschwitz, Dachau, Bergen Belsen, and Buchenwald have. Yet for sheer unrelieved brutality it may well have surpassed them all. At no other camp did the commander give prisoners to his young son for target practice.

Ziereis' Final Statement[8]

I, Franz Ziereis, make the following statement of my own free will. Born in Munich, 13th August 1905, my father was born 12th July, 1868, killed in battle in 1916. Mother Caroline (Schrobesberger) was born 12th September, 1862, in Bavaria. One brother, two sisters. In the Reichswehr in the 19th Bavarian Infantry Regiment from 1st April, 1924, until September 30, 1936. Came out as First Lt. 30th September 1936, entered as Obersturmführer and training officer in the Waffen SS (i.e., into the 4th SS Standarte in Oranienburg) when I left these and as SS Hauptsturmführer was made the successor of the former commandant Sauer at concentration camp Mauthausen. After two years, in 1941, was promoted to Sturmbannführer. In 1943 to Obersturmbannführer and finally in 1944 to Standartenführer. Repeatedly volunteered for front. The SS men/prisoner ratio was 1:10. The garrison at Mauthausen consisted of SS Totenkopf, from which it is necessary to make two differentiations. About 4–5,000 members of this SS must be considered as storm troopers of the Totenkopf, the rest, about 5–600 former army and airforce personnel.

Glücks ordered the destruction of documents which was begun at the end of April. Upon request of the Reichsführer SS drafted prisoners into the SS to give them a chance to redeem themselves, particularly in the fight against Russia. These men numbered some 450 in Mauthausen and Gusen. Most of them volunteered, though some were chosen by the leaders of the protective custody camp. Blames Bachmayer for deaths. In November 1940, 320 Poles shot in Mauthausen by order of Heydrich. Admitted taking part in shooting of prisoners because "in his opinion, the SS shot too badly!" Used small calibre rifle. In a room there was arranged a music loudspeaker and behind a screen was a machine-gun which would kill prisoners when they entered the room. He did this. The insane and incurable professional criminals etc., were sent to Hartheim near Linz by order of Lonauer and Renault. Transfers were signed by both. We were told to report those who had died at Hartheim as having died naturally at Mauthausen. Krebsach blamed for death car. Some thousands were murdered by Seidler in Gusen. Out of Bachmayer's murders about ⅔ were committed by SS Hauptsturmführer Spatzenegger. Gruppenführer Müller and Kaltenbrunner signed the certificates from Group D. Seidler and Chmielewski had book covers and screens made from human skin. It was forbidden but he did not interfere. Chmielewski has shot and killed several thousand human beings. In February 1945, an order came from Pohl that in case of a bad end of the war all prisoners were to be driven into the woods to pick flowers and buds. Mauthausen last camp into which Auschwitz prisoners came, Dachau and Buchenwald etc. by the thousands without prior knowledge. Each transport had about 6–800 dead without counting those who were tossed out of the train en route. Order not to provide Mauthausen with food came from the Food Director. 4,800 prisoners arrived in April, of which only 180 survived, the rest were shot whilst trying to escape.

In April, Himmler said in Vienna, that if any trouble occurred in camps, it would be answered with dismissal of commandants. Obersturmbannführer Lorenz was killed by partisans in Italy. He liquidated a whole typhus camp. Later on he liquidated Austler camp in Weiwers. This was situated in Poland. Herbert was ordered by Himmler to transform the Warsaw Ghetto into a lawn. Himmler later sentenced him to death for misappropriation of Jewish property. Schuetz was transferred to Auschwitz because of thefts and after being convicted was shot there. Stolen in Auschwitz too. Lechebush from the SS Economics office had bought merchandise in France and carried out trade with the Poles. At Katowice, he was given to understand he must shoot himself, which he did. He said that in the brothel he set up cine camera to detect any illegal passing of messages during sexual intercourse. The charge for each visit to brothel was Reichsmark 1.50 (and those men who had been sterilized were expected to continue intercourse as long as possible). He formed a regiment in which he put his SS men. Six companies were disarmed by the Americans near the east exit of Mauthausen, rifles, bazookas etc., were thrown into the Danube and then the men marched in close formation to Mauthausen. Watched all this through field glasses and saw how Seidler and Obermayer surrendered to the U.S. No shots were fired by this battalion. The second battalion was captured too and Dr. Rab had his troops disarmed also after he escaped. The battalion was taken prisoner between St. Peter and Haag.

He (Ziereis) said he would shoot the rascal Himmler also Pohl and said that Hitler was a political adventurer who told a lot of nonsense. Formerly he received 600 rm salary and 300 rm from DEST. One SS man went with two tanks to fight through the US lines. He had 25 SS men from the staff and suffered heavy losses.

The V.I. (Doodlebug) middle joint length 12 m was built in the Raxworks at Wiener Neustadt and the body was then changed. The matter was then betrayed through the employment of foreign workers in Redyl-Zipf (Schlier) where two proving stands were for fuel for filling of V.2. In Redyl-Zipf there was a secret printing plant of the RSHA which had one dpt. for the production of counterfeit dollars, pounds, francs etc, but unfortunately this money was used by the traitors for their flight. He saw 150 boxes 1 m long 15 cms high and 50 cm deep, full of counterfeit money. Prisoners there under Kruger. Work supervised by Hantsch, from S of the RSHA. He had orders that if the US approached to move the material to Ebensee in order to continue producing money and passes. In printing plant 150 Jews, all lithographers, were employed.   Sgd. FRANZ ZIEREIS

1. See J. Presser, *The Destruction of the Dutch Jews* (New York, 1969).
2. Rodney Minott, *The Fortress That Never Was* (New York, 1964).
3. Evelyn Le Chêne, *Mauthausen: The History of a Death Camp* (London, 1971).
4. *Ibid.*
5. *Ibid.*, p. 157.
6. George Dyer, 12th Corps, *Spearhead of Patton's Third Army* (Germany, 1947).
7. Le Chêne, pp. 170–171.
8. *Ibid.*, pp. 171–174.

THERESIENSTADT

Introduction

The last camp to be liberated was Theresienstadt, and its liberation presented a number of unusual characteristics. First, Theresienstadt was a "model" camp and as such was organized and run, on the surface at least, on a different basis than the other camps. It was a Jewish camp, not in the accidental sense that Bergen-Belsen became one, but so designated from the beginning by the SS.[1] Himmler told Dr. Norbert Masur of the World Jewish Congress that "Theresienstadt is not a camp in the ordinary sense of the word but a town inhabited by Jews and governed by them and in which every manner of work is done. This type of camp was designed by me and my friend Heydrich and so we intended all camps to be."[2] Himmler's description of Theresienstadt is inaccurate in every particular except his assertion that it was not a camp "in the ordinary sense of the word." In some ways it was worse, in some ways better than the other camps, but it was unique in being a camp exclusively for Jews. Finally, Theresienstadt was unique in the way that it was liberated. On May 2, 1945, the German commandant turned the camp over to a representative of the International Red Cross and he in turn gave the camp over to the Russians 10 days later. The camp, then, was not so much liberated as put under international control.

Prior History of the Camp[3]

On November 24, 1941, Heydrich ordered the fortress city of Theresienstadt cleared of its inhabitants in preparation for the arrival of Jews from the Protectorate. At first, he only thought in terms of making Theresienstadt a transfer camp where Jews would be housed for a relatively short period of time before being transferred East. However, at the Wannsee Conference held on January 20, 1942, Heydrich announced his intention to make Theresienstadt into a model camp for "privileged" Jews, privileged being defined as decorated war veterans, prominents of one sort or another with international reputations, etc. and later those who could pay to be put in these categories. From the opening of the camp in 1942 until the end of 1944 the population of the camp fluctuated from 10,000 to 60,000. There was a constant and heavy flow of Jews into and out of the camp. Some of those who arrived at the "model" camp were shipped sooner or later to Auschwitz and almost certain death; others remained in the camp where short rations, hard work, and desperate overcrowding took a terrible toll. In 1942, for example, 88,000 Jews were transferred to Theresienstadt and of that number 30,000 died there while 7,000 more were shipped to Auschwitz, leaving some 49,000 inmates in the camp at the end of the year. In the autumn of 1944 the inflow all but stopped and outflow to Auschwitz increased dramatically with the result that by the beginning of 1945 the population of the camp was not much more than 10,000—still crowded but a far cry from the average of nearly 60,000 in 1942–1943.[4]

As the war drew to a close, various relief agencies worked to save as many lives as possible of those in the camps. These rescue efforts were in large measure concentrated on assisting the inmates of Theresienstadt.[5] The first small victory was won in February 1945 when Himmler authorized the transfer of 1,200 Jews from Theresienstadt to Switzerland.[6] The train that carried the inmates had Pullman cars, and the fortunate passengers were given such unheard of luxuries as cakes, chocolate, and marmalade as they travelled to safety. Two months went by before any further successes were achieved. Then on April 6, 1945, the SS allowed M. Paul Dunand, a Swiss Red Cross official, to visit Theresienstadt, not to negotiate for the release of prisoners, but to check on conditions in the camp and to gain assurances that no last minute mass executions would take place.[7] For the occasion the camp was tidied up, a bogus kindergarten was trotted out, fake shops set up; in short, every effort was made to give the camp the appearance of a "normal" city. Dunand was accompanied by Eichmann, and after the inspection a formal reception was held during which Dunand was assured that the Jews in Theresienstadt would be safe. A few days later, however, Dunand learned that the SS records had been destroyed, and fearing that this might well be a prelude to a mass execution Dunand hurried to Berlin where he obtained new assurances from the Gestapo Chief Heinrich Mueller. Whether there was a plan to wipe out the ghetto or not is unclear, but if there was, Dunand apparently forestalled it.

The Germans permitted a second delivery of inmates to the Red Cross on April 15, 1945; this time Danish and Norwegian Jews were put under the aegis of the Swedish Red Cross. The departure caused, as can be imagined, great excitement in the camp. An SS informer's report gives a graphic description of the event.

> With the departure of the Danes the Ghetto was in an uproar. When it was learned that the Swedish Red Cross was providing buses for the transport of the Danish Jews the feeling in the Ghetto was—as you can imagine—that the end of the Ghetto was only a matter of hours.
>
> The over-optimistic even packed their bags... For the inhabitants of the Ghetto it was a sensation that Jews had been allowed to leave the Ghetto as a result of negotiations with the German government. The departure of the buses was a sight well worth seeing. Especially in that the people recognized the generosity of the camp administration in that those remaining behind were allowed to go up to the buses... That evening there was a great unrest and the numbers on the streets was exceptionally large. There were rumors of all sorts... Between midnight and one in the morning the cry was heard that the Ghetto was free. "The Commission has taken over. We are under the protection of the Geneva convention." This rumor spread like wildfire.[8]

The rumor proved to be false, and morale sank as rations were cut and somewhere between 13,500 and 15,000 prisoners from other camps were dumped into Theresienstadt—some Jews and some gentiles, all weary, hungry, and most sick. Buildings CIII and HV were cleared and the new arrivals were put into quarantine.[9] On April 24 the first cases of typhus were reported and before the month was out the number of victims was in the thousands. One of the long-time inmates described the new arrivals.

> In the course of the night two transports arrived. Yes, evacuated from "strict" concentration camps. They aren't men any more, they are wild animals. Animals who for weeks have had nothing to eat... For three years they have known only gas chambers, flaming chimneys, shootings, and beatings... One transport in open cars. Seventeen days![10]

Liberation

At the end of April Dunand again visited the camp, and the German commandant, Obersturmführer Karl Rahm, unofficially turned the camp over to the Swiss Red Cross. Three days later the government of the Protectorate gave their approval to the *fait accompli*. The inmates were not immediately aware of the change that had taken place. A female inmate reported:

> Something had disappeared, the Swastika, the sign of our terrible humiliation was not hanging any more from the Rathaus tower. And soon it was spoken everywhere. The whisper was a certain truth, that instead of the Swastika, the flag of the Red Cross had been raised. Mr. Dunand, the representative of that great organization, had succeeded in getting the leadership of the prison camp into his hands. The danger of gassing ended.

Another inmate recalled the moment she became aware that she was free:

> One thinks that nothing had happened. That all is as it had been. One ventures forward. Looking toward all sides one goes a few steps. And looks and is astonished and understands it not: Nowhere can a German uniform be seen. No guards; no watchers ... The Germans have fled. Unobserved. The Germans have gone! They have fled!

Dunand, in effect, turned the camp over to a council of elders. He was proud that in the few days that he was in control only two inmates died violent deaths—one killed by random firing of German troops retreating from the Russians and one killed by a Russian shell—and equally proud of the fact that there was no mass flight from the camp, something he was powerless to prevent, and which could have had tragic consequences for all concerned. Dunand asked Leo Baeck and several other prominent Jews to head the camp. Baeck, a man with a world-wide reputation as a scholar, was highly revered by the inmates. H. G. Adler, a survivor, wrote:

> The most memorable personality in the council of the Elders was Rabbi Leo Baeck ... who was universally respected among all prisoners and regarded with even higher esteem for his readiness to help. He never withdrew from the camp, but it did not seem to exist near him; none of the filth could touch him. Peace emanated from him. He could be gentle but he could also speak with zealous anger, for he knew the demand of the hour, knew the fateful failings to which he and everyone else in the framework of history was subject ... he was a shining beacon in the salt-tear ocean of despair.[11]

Baeck and his colleages issued the following proclamation to the inmates on May 6, 1945.

> Men and Women of Theresienstadt!
> The International Committee of the Red Cross has undertaken the protection of Theresienstadt. The representative of this committee, Herr Dunand, has been appointed leader of

Theresienstadt. He has entrusted the undersigned members of the existing council of elders with the leadership of the self-government.

In Theresienstadt you are safe. The war is still not ended! Those of you who might leave Theresienstadt expose yourselves to many dangers.

Theresienstadt has undertaken the care of the martyred of the small fortress. This means increased work, which also is necessary for the preparation of the transportation back.

Mail now is permitted in any language, without censorship and without any other restriction. For the introduction of this postal service every resident of Theresienstadt, who wishes, will receive a franked postcard, to the extent that a sufficient number is available.

Newspapers will be received and will be posted so all can read them. Seriously ill persons still are present here, meaning that a strong observation of the quarantine rules is necessary. For that reason, observe them carefully.

When the war ends, the transports back will begin promptly and then authorities will begin issuing out instructions for the handling of the return.

Obey rules and laws! Help us with our work, the return home shall be made possible. Go each of you to your designated work place.[12]

On the evening of May 7, 1945, Russian tanks arrived, and the inmates then knew that liberation was a fact. An inmate told of the Russians distributing cigarettes, tobacco, bread, and sugar to the inmates; of wild celebrations that lasted all night long—a night turned into day by the numerous campfires; of laughing, drinking, and singing; of going out to the nearby highway to watch the broken Wehrmacht plod down the roads to prison camps. But at the end of her description of a day of boundless joy she noted—a not uncharacteristic remark—"... the world is so empty and the future before us so desolate."[13]

In the hours between the departure of the SS and the arrival of the Russians, Karl Rahm was the last to leave, a bureaucrat to the end. He rode on a bicycle from gate to gate locking them and collecting keys. Order must be maintained. The Jews watched him silently. Leo Baeck watched this strange scene and then turned to a companion and said, "Look at it. This can only happen with Jews. Of all these Jewish people here, not one person lifted a stone to throw at him. They could have strangled him if they wanted."[14] In recounting this incident Leonard Baker commented, "Jews believed that vengeance is taken away from man by God, that man has no right to vengeance. After the Nazi barbarity, they still believed that—that was the ultimate triumph of the Jews at Theresienstadt."

An American correspondent, Meyer Levin, reached Theresienstadt on May 10, 1945. Five years later he was moved to write an autobiography which he said was "about being a Jew." His comments on Theresienstadt at the moment of liberation are worth quoting in extenso.

Now we began to visit Theresienstadt. Though this was the best—if one can use such a word—of the concentration camps, it was nevertheless a place of death; no children were permitted to be born; the community was there to die. Periodically there were levies of men and women for the slave camps. The remainder passed through their days on a starvation diet, counting out their last trinkets in trades to the guards for additional food. My guide told me how her own baby had died. She had come to the camp with her husband and their little girl, a year old. She had brought no clothes for herself, only this dress she wore, in order to bring all of her baby's things, and her baby had become the idol of the camp. "I kept her always in white. I washed her clothes incessantly, bargained away everything I had so that I might keep her as well as though we were outside. Can you understand? It seemed to me that if I succeeded in this one thing, in keeping my baby properly, it would be the symbol for everything. Oh, in this whole dreary camp, she was the liveliest, the prettiest thing, so fresh, so white, so dainty, through her we knew we were still human beings."

And then? After some months the baby had begun to weaken for lack of fresh food. It sickened and died.

The mother looked at me, with blank uncomprehension still in her, and I saw that she was half mad from the experience. She hadn't been able to save her child, nobody had been able to save the child in this place. And somehow her tragedy seemed more terrible than that of the mothers who went into the gas chambers with their babies clutched to their breasts.

This was the "soft" concentration camp, a slow distillation of death; yet after all for some thirty thousand it had meant survival. But nothing was unpaid for in Europe, and their survival contained a final diabolism. For these inhabitants of Theresienstadt survived through considering themselves superior to the verminous "eastern Jews" who had been exterminated in the slave camps and the crematoria.

Again it may be felt that such things as I have to tell here should be kept "amongst ourselves" in the Jewish world. But this is more than a book about Jews; it seeks to touch the human spirit, and my Jewish experience is the probe. Therefore I must relate that when I came into Theresienstadt I found a ghetto within a ghetto.

For in the center of this little walled village there were two buildings, guarded, their windows covered with barbed wire to prevent escape. Inside those buildings were Jews who had arrived in the last weeks from Buchenwald and Dachau, the Jews who had survived the last trip in locked evacuation trains.

100

The Nazis, in a final act of cynicism, had shipped them here. The trains had arrived, such trains as I had seen at the gates of Dachau—boxcars bedded several deep with the corpses of those who had died en route, and the survivors on top of them. The survivors were typhus ridden and a danger to the clean community of Theresienstadt, that was true. They were therefore herded into two hastily vacated barracks and segregated there behind barbed wire.

Walking into those barracks was like walking again through lower Buchenwald. The survirors lay on the bare floors, or limped half dead through the sloshy-filthy corridors. There were a few common washrooms with troughs along the walls, and an inadequate dribble of water that nevertheless was not drained off, and on the floors of those washrooms they had retched out the last of their sick insides.

As I passed through the dim crowded little rooms some of the survivors, still conscious enough to realize that an American had appeared, seized me, screaming, "Look what they have done with us! Our own Jews! They are treating us worse than the Germans did in Buchenwald!" A skeletal wraith lying on the floor grasped my feet and gasped at me, "I have typhus! There is no doctor, there is no one for us!"

There were women also in this heap of filth, all were mingled together; in the hallway a young girl passed me, a dark little girl of perhaps seventeen with huge supernatural black eyes and an ineffable beauty that I have never since been able to forget. She was carrying water to someone, in a tin can.

We came out of that depth of hell, and my guide led me to the Theresienstadt hospital. It was quiet, clean, excellently equipped, for the able practitioners of Prague and Vienna and Berlin had been permitted to bring their instruments and part of their medical machinery here, and the hospital was of course staffed with some of the finest physicians and surgeons of three countries. There were vacant beds in every ward.

We emerged into the courtyard, and just then a wagon drove through an archway: it carried the daily ration of bread. A husky young woman stood on the wagon to carry out the distribution, but she was helpless. The vehicle was instantly mobbed, and from all corners the mob increased; we were caught in it as the ravenous survivors, oblivious of the shrieks of women trampled upon, or of cries from the camp police for order, unheeding to any appeal or command, raged and tore at each other to reach the wagon. We fought our way backward to get out of the crowd, and managed to escape up a stairway. The wagon was already empty.

The soup distribution, my guide told me, was still managed with some degree of control, but since there was no assurance of further supplies the inmates were frantic with fear. The "east Jews" had broken into the potato cellars and cleaned them out.

We returned toward the administration building. Erik yelled

to me from the jeep.

In the front seat sat a frail white-haired woman with a white nursecap on her head. He had found his mother.[15]

On May 10, 1945, the Russian military officially took over the camp. By June there were only 5,000-odd prisoners left, and before the end of the year the camp was empty.

1. H. G. Adler, *Theresienstadt 1941–1945: Das Anlitz Einer Zwangsgemeinschaft* (Tübingen, 1960) p. 16.
2. *Ibid.,* p. 22.
3. *Ibid.,* pp. 16–36. See also Adler, *Der Verhainlichte Wahrheit: Theresienstadter Dokumente* (Tübingen, 1958).
4. On January 1, 1942, there were 7,365 inmates in the camp. At the end of the year 91,373 Jews were transported to the camp and 43,871 were deported to the death camps in the East.
5. See Red Cross, *Documents dur l'activite du comite international de la Croix-Rouge en faveur des civils detenus dans les camps de concentration en Allemagne* (Geneva, 1947).
6. Adler, p. 200.
7. *Ibid.,* p. 203.
8. *Ibid.,* p. 209 ff.
9. *Ibid.,* pp. 211–212.
10. *Ibid.,* pp. 213–314.
11. *Ibid.*
12. *Ibid.,* pp. 215–216.
13. *Ibid.,* p. 217.
14. *Ibid.*
15. Meyer Levin, *In Search: An Autobiography* (New York, 1950) pp. 277 ff.

CONCLUSION

The liberation of the Western camps affected post-war politics and attitudes in two quite separate ways. First, the opening of the camps in April and May 1945, making as it did such a powerful emotional impact on the conscience of the West, left in its wake a number of misconceptions. These misconceptions in their turn have been in some measure responsible for revisionist theories concerning both the fact of genocide and its ultimate meaning. Second, the very drama of liberation had the result of setting post-war attitudes towards Jews and what used to be called the "Jewish Question." These immediate responses have, of course, undergone significant modifications as the event recedes into the past, but they have never been completely effaced and still influence national policies and popular attitudes.

Popular Misconceptions

In the immediate aftermath of the liberation of the camps in Western Europe most people believed that genocide was practiced only at Bergen-Belsen, Dachau and Buchenwald. This mistaken impression has led to a blurring of the distinction between a death camp and a concentration camp. To be sure, specialists suffer no confusion, but even such a respected text as Winks, Brinton, Christopher and Wolff gives a remarkably muddied account of the whole business in which Auschwitz is identified as a concentration camp and victims of the epidemics that swept through the camps in the last days of the war are labeled "victims of genocide."

These errors and many more like them are not of much consequence in the sense that they do not obscure the larger truth of the murderous policy of the National Socialist regime, but as the years have passed these errors have tangentially added fuel to two revisionist arguments. First, the right-wing revisionists use these errors as a means of casting doubt on the fact of genocide. They contend that the Jewish conspiracy has cleverly used the fact that a few thousand Jews died of disease in the camps to create a completely mythical massacre of millions.[1] The evidence for genocide, however, is so overwhelming that only the most fanatic choose to deny it.

In sharp contrast, the left revisionists are perfectly respectable historians who make a strong but debatable case. They have spawned popularizers, however, who seem little interested in the subtleties of the argument and have indiscriminately branded Roosevelt, Churchill and their major advisors, with a very few exceptions, as guilty of aiding and abetting genocide.[2] In part, the passionate conviction of this group gains credibility because in a sense "liberation" can be viewed as a fraud. The argument runs something like this: "They told us the Americans and British saved the remnant of the European Jewish communities when they liberated the camps, but they failed to point out that the overwhelming percentage of victims were killed in the East where neither the Americans or the British lifted a finger to save them."

The initial misconceptions about liberation have been corrected over the years, but some historians, including textbook writers who should know better, remain unaware that the initial story needs considerable modification. A minority, however, when they found that the 1945 accounts were in many details wrong have drawn their own conclusions from this fact—the right revisionists that it never happened; the left that the Allies were major contributors to the destruction of the European Jews. I cannot emphasize enough that these comments are not in any sense directed at such historians as Martin Gilbert and his classic study *Auschwitz and the Allies,* but relate rather to those who vulgarize his arguments and those of other historians using them to denigrate the entire British-American war effort.

In the popular mind, the liberation of the camps was and always will be indelibly connected with the end of genocide. And while this is true in the sense that the 75,000 surviving Jews in camps were rescued from almost certain death, it obscures the fact that the overwhelming majority of the "remnant" of European Jews numbering more than one million who survived did so because the Allied armies defeated Germany, and not because the camps were liberated. Had Hitler won the war, those million survivors would surely have been killed sooner or later. The American, British and Russian soldiers who died to destroy

Naziism were responsible for saving what remained of the European Jewish community. In 1945 this seemed obvious. In those heady days no one was churlish enough to suggest that the Allies were, by some contortion of moral logic, responsible for genocide.

On Roosevelt's death, American Jewish leaders were unanimous in their praise of the man who "led the country to victory against the forces of darkness." He was described as a man of "unbounded sympathy" for the plight of the victims of Hitler and his regime. When the war ended Jewish leaders were unstinting in their praise of the American armed forces and its leaders. In a sermon preached on August 16, 1945, Rabbi Nathan Perilman said, "We must remain ever mindful of those who served so nobly in behalf of *the causes* for which we have been fighting the war."[3] (Emphasis added. N. b. Jewish leaders in 1945 were very reluctant to single out the saving of European Jews as *the* cause for which the war was fought.) And they freely acknowledged that there were many victims of Hitler's bloodlust other than Jews.

It is true that in 1944 international Jewish organizations had pleaded with the Allies to launch air assaults on Auschwitz in an effort to stop or at least retard the last terrible act of genocide, the destruction of the Hungarian Jews. But when their petitions were rejected, most of them loyally accepted the argument that such attacks were unlikely to be effective and might even lead to the death of thousands of those they were designed to help—or at least the Jewish organizations did not raise the issue after the war, being unwilling to embarrass their governments. The argument that victory stopped genocide was almost universally accepted in 1945.

It was only in the 1970s, when memories began to fade and archives were opened, that the case was made that the Allies could have saved many more Jews but failed to do so. So heated has the rhetoric become that the unwary reader of some of the extreme examples of historical self-flagellation might conclude that the Germans were little more than innocent by-standers while the real perpetrators of the crime were the British and Americans, and that Roosevelt and Churchill should properly have been standing in the dock of history along with Adolf Hitler and Heinrich Himmler. In part the revisionists base their argument on the now well-documented fact that neither Churchill, Roosevelt nor any of their top advisors, with a few exceptions like Henry Morgenthau, showed more than a casual interest in any scheme put forth by desperate Jewish leaders to save their brethren in Europe. Time and again, so the argument runs, such pleas were passed on to underlings who allowed them to disappear in a bureaucratic maze. This cavalier attitude does not read very well in retrospect, and it is made more unsavory by the occasional but unmistakable marginal comments which smack of anti-semitism.[4] The historical record makes it all too clear that the British and Americans believed that only victory would end the killing of the European Jews as well as all the other victims of National Socialism, and any action which diverted forces from that goal was not to be considered.

The case against rescue operations, though often made with little concern for the sensitivity of those who proposed the plans, was, for all that, a powerful one. Bombing the railroads to Auschwitz was so fraught with difficulties that even those most anxious to condemn the American actions concede that it was probably not feasible.[5] As for bombing the gas chambers themselves a better case can be made; the gas chambers probably could have been destroyed. But this is largely beside the point. Hitler put the highest possible priority on the destruction of the Jews. Time and again even the most pressing military needs were given a lower priority than killing Jews. The gas chambers, even if destroyed, could have been easily replaced. If the Germans were able to rebuild something as complex as their hydrogenation plants despite repeated raids, it makes no sense at all to imagine that they could not construct three or four airtight rooms. But even if they could not, Jews did not have to be killed by gas; in 1941 the Einsatzgruppe had murdered a million Jews in a matter of a few months using nothing more sophisticated than machine guns. Hitler was perfectly capable of reverting to such primitive methods. The destruction of the Hungarian Jews in 1944 might have been somewhat slowed but hardly stopped, no matter what measures the Allies took.

Liberation of the camps then did not save more than 5–10 percent of the European Jews who remained alive on May 8, 1945. That fact was not fully appreciated in 1945, and it was at least in part because of the mistaken impressions created by the liberation of the camps that the revisionist works of the 1970s and beyond have become rooted in the popular mind. By 1944 the average newspaper reader in the West knew that Hitler was slaughtering vast numbers of Jews. By the end of the year, the figure 6,000,000 had already gained some currency. The evidence for what would later be called "genocide" was so wide-ranging, so pervasive, and came from so many apparently unimpeachable sources that even a hardened skeptic would have been hard-pressed to find any grounds to doubt the fact of the Holocaust.

The details, however, were quite another matter. The methods, places and times were confused and always somewhat fuzzy. In 1944 the very name "Auschwitz" was known only to a few top officials but as yet had no resonance at all in the popular mind while the very existence of Belzec and Treblinka was unsuspected. Then came the liberation after which most people jumped to the conclusion that Dachau, Bergen-Belsen and Buchenwald were, in fact, the death camps. One can hardly emphasize strongly enough that none of the scholars or even popular historians who have written of the Holocaust are in any way confused in their own minds about what happened, but I think a good case can be made that the ready popular acceptance of the revisionist position may in part be explained by popular errors rooted in the liberation drama.

The first pictures of the liberation of the camps, with their horrifying scenes of the dead and dying strewn across the central roll-call areas of the camps and pits filled with skeletal remains, are etched forever in the conscience of the civilized world. Here was graphic evidence of the total evil of the National Socialist world; if anyone doubted the justice of the Allied cause, the pictures offered irrefutable proof to the contrary. But looking back on the pictures and their accompanying captions, it is clear they created a number of false impressions. First and foremost, the pictures strongly suggested that genocide was going on in the liberated camps. In fact, genocide was ended by order of Himmler in November 1944. As a result of the order, the gas chambers were closed down, their systematic destruction begun and the remaining inmates prepared for transfer to the West.

It is true that in the six months between the giving of the order to stop genocide and the end of the war, tens of thousands of Jews died at the hands of the Germans: some from over-work, some from disease, some from the brutality of the guards. One could plausibly argue that these deaths were simply genocide by other means, but such a claim tends to obscure the unique nature of genocide in three ways.

First, genocide was directed at a specific group—the Jews—with the objective of their total annihilation. The deaths that occurred after genocide per se ended claimed their victims with a growing randomness. True, Jews were inevitably singled out for the worst treatment, but in the growing chaos of the last weeks when the most rudimentary elements of order collapsed in the camps even the SS lost the ability to single out its victims. The diseases that killed so many in the last days were even-handed and even the Kapos and the occasional SS man fell victim to them.

Secondly, genocide was the official policy of the German government carried out with the cooperation of dozens of different bureaucratic units and thousands of functionaries. The catastrophe which overwhelmed the camps in the last weeks was not the result of any policy decision; indeed, the government had largely lost the ability to implement any policy at all, as increasingly it was every man for himself. Hitler in his bunker issued orders but his underlings no longer felt any obligation to obey any orders except those which they thought might benefit them. So Himmler, Goering, and Speer all set out on independent courses as did most of the concentration camp commanders. Hitler ordered all inmates of the camps to be killed; Himmler countermanded the order; the commandants acted for the most part to save their own skins. The policy of genocide led to the death of 6 million

Jews; the number of post-genocide victims is impossible to estimate with any degree of accuracy but it surely was not more than 1–2 percent of that figure. Using the analogy of criminal law the 6 million were the victims of premeditated murder in the first degree without any conceivable mitigating circumstances. The deaths of the post-genocide victims could, in the criminal law analogy, in many cases be classified as murder, but in other cases aggravated manslaughter would be more appropriate. Put another way, had Hitler's major crime been the post-genocide victims, the historical reputation of the regime would surely be considerably different than it is now. For genocide more than anything else distinguishes the Hitlerian regime from other brutal regimes before and after. Of course, none of this should be interpreted as in any way condoning or finding excuses for the post-genocide deaths. It is merely necessary to distinguish the two cases. In the first edition of *Commentary* the editors eloquently argued that ". . . as Jews, we live with this fact: 4,750,000 of 6,000,000 Jews of Europe have been murdered. Not killed in battle, not massacred in hot blood, but slaughtered like cattle, subjected to every physical indignity— processed."[6]

Initially, then, the liberation of the Western camps fostered the impression that liberation ended genocide. Beyond that the liberation planted the idea in many peoples' minds that the survivors in the camps were indeed the only survivors, while in fact, less than 5 percent of those who survived were among the liberated. In 1933 the total Jewish population of Europe was estimated to be 9.5 million. Of those, 1.5 million lived in lands which never came under German control and were thus never directly threatened; rather more than one million managed to emigrate to safe havens; about 6 million were killed and approximately one million survived in areas under German dominion but were never picked up. How did one million Jews manage to escape the SS? Some were in resistance; some were harbored by friendly Gentiles; some hid; but most were in states like Bulgaria, Denmark, Rumania, etc., which for whatever reason were reluctant to cooperate with the policy of genocide. Had the Germans been victorious it is difficult to believe that many of this million would have long survived. Victory then, not liberation, was in the main responsible for the surviving "remnant."

The third and final misconception which the freeing of the camps fostered was the not unnatural idea that the Germans were totally responsible for the destruction of the European Jews. Of course, no one would deny the primary responsibility of the Germans for the crime of genocide, but they were aided and abetted by local fascist organizations like the Arrow Cross in Hungary and the Iron Guard in Rumania as well as by a number of satellite governments whose attitude ranged from reluctant compliance to zealous haste in complying with the demands of the Germans to turn over their Jews. But all that was more or less realized at the time; more to the point is the guilt of Stalin.

To be sure, the Soviet Union not only did not carry out anything that could be remotely described as "extermination" of the Jews, and indeed the Soviet government officially opposed the racist policies of the Germans; and indeed Soviet Jewish citizens served in the Red Army, many rising to high rank. But for all that hundreds of thousands of Jews died or were murdered in the Soviet Union from 1941 to 1945. Some died in slave labor camps; some died when being moved to the interior after the German invasion; some were executed for various political crimes. Jews as Jews were not killed but the fact remains they suffered more than any other group. For example, in 1940 there were somewhere between 50,000 and 100,000 Jews living in Northern Bukovina and Bessarabia when those areas were annexed to the Soviet Union; these Jews were deported to the interior of the Soviet Union and most were never heard from again. The same fate awaited the Polish Jews who lived in those eastern portions of Poland annexed by Russia in 1939. Again most were taken East; again few survived. True, had those Jews remained in their homes when the Germans arrived none would have survived, but conceding that, the mindless brutality of the Stalinist regime still was responsible for the deaths of large numbers of Jews. In 1945, however, it was psychologically difficult for many people in the West, including many Jews, to tar Stalin with the same brush as Hitler, so it followed that Stalin's admittedly lesser crimes were largely forgotten.

One of the lasting results of the liberation of the camps happening in the way that it did was to imprint on the collective mind of the West images which are hard to efface. Though these images are in a general way true they do have some tendency to distort reality. The right-wing revisionists who hint that genocide never happened have used these distortions to cast doubts on the very existence of genocide; the left-wing revisionists have gained a wider audience than they would perhaps have had were there not so much muddle in the popular mind about genocide, the Final Solution and extermination.

Attitudes Towards Liberation

The liberation of the camps—which for most people represented the first absolutely incontrovertible proof that the Germans had committed crimes of such magnitude and such an unspeakable nature that they did not even have a name—elicited four distinct responses. First, the victorious powers of the West were moved to take unprecedented actions in order to make some compensation for the survivors. Against all conventional wisdom the leaders of the United States and Great

Britain embarked—rather tepidly it is true—on policies of special treatment which in the pre-war world would have been considered politically suicidal. And the common man in the democracies accepted almost without demure the idea that Jews had suffered the most and should rightly be compensated. This remarkable *volte face*, it should be emphasized, was much more the product of liberation than of genocide itself. In other words, during the war when genocide was only a hazy reality special treatment was anathema, but the pictures of Bergen-Belsen, Dachau and the rest more than anything created an entirely new climate of opinion. In sharp contrast, the leaders of the Soviet Union, for complex ideological and political reasons, almost never acknowledged that such a thing as the Holocaust happened. Among the crimes of the National Socialist party the attempted extermination of European Jewry is omitted from all official Soviet publications. Monuments to the "Victims of Fascism" abound but Jews as such are never listed as victims.

As for the Germans, most seemed indifferent in the immediate aftermath of the catastrophe of 1945 and remain so today. Indeed, many seem outright hostile if the subject is broached. From a human standpoint this attitude is perfectly understandable, for after all most Germans had little or nothing to do with the crimes of Hitler and anyway, "what has happened has happened and nothing can be done about it now." At some level, however, there is great uneasiness about the national past, but it only rarely comes to the surface.

Finally, in the Far East genocide, the Holocaust, the liberation and all the rest never made a significant impact on the population. The whole affair seemed remote and largely inconsequential. This attitude prevails today and is exemplified by two small but telling examples. First, *Mein Kampf* is readily available in bookstores all over the Far East and is sold without embarrassment. Second, bars with National Socialist themes (swastikas, pictures of Hitler, etc.) are by no means unknown. And the average person in Japan, Korea, or Hong Kong not only finds nothing particularly strange about this, but is baffled by Western sensitivity to what to him seems little more than a historical oddity.

The British and Americans hailed the liberation of the camps as a proper and fitting capstone to their war effort. From the very beginning they had proclaimed that they were fighting against the evil of Naziism which if it triumphed would usher in "a New Dark Age made more sinister by perverted science." Liberation provided overwhelming evidence that the "New Dark Age" was no mere figure of speech. The deaths in battle of American and British soldiers were then invested with a kind of sanctity: after the opening of the camps who could say that they died in vain?

Ironically, during the war the salvation of the European Jews was rarely put forth as a major war aim, and it was only after the end of the war that the Allies increasingly claimed—retrospectively—that the salvation of the Jews had been their primary aim from the beginning. The reluctance of Churchill and Roosevelt to identify their cause too closely with that of the Jews came from a lurking anxiety that anti-semitism was a powerful if latent force in their own societies and that nothing should be done to rouse it. Up to 1945, mildly anti-semitic jokes, dimissive remarks, restrictive covenants, quotas of one sort or another were commonly accepted as normal even among the well-educated classes in England, the United States and Canada. It was widely predicted even by well-respected commentators such as George Orwell that as soon as the war was over anti-semitism would assume a more vicious form.

But in fact even relatively mild forms of anti-semitism became passé in the postwar world. The liberation undoubtedly played more than a little role in this surprising shift in popular attitude. Many people became convinced that even supposedly innocent remarks were no longer acceptable in the post-liberation world. There was even a growing feeling that the world actually owed the survivors something after what they had endured.

In the Soviet Union the liberation of the camps was all but a non-event. From 1941 to his death in 1953 Stalin never publicly mentioned the Jews; Soviet accounts of the war contain only the briefest passing references to genocide; Soviet official publications describing Majdanek and Auschwitz never mention that the principal victims were Jews. Even the part played by the Soviet Jews in the war was seldom mentioned and this despite the fact that Jews as a racial group suffered a higher casualty rate than Great Russians and won more medals per thousand to boot. Neither Stalin nor the Soviet hierarchy made any mention of these facts nor did they make any effort to refute the commonly repeated canards that most Jews had somehow managed to escape combat. When the Russians liberated Lublin they gave the story ample publicity but were careful not to say or imply that the majority of the victims were Jews. After the liberation of Auschwitz their attitude could only be described as cryptic, for they refused for five months even to admit that the camp existed. In the West liberation meant the end of the Holocaust; to the Russians the existence of the Holocaust was barely acknowledged. When Jews returning to their homes in the Ukraine tried to reclaim their property, they were met with hostility and on occasion physical violence. While the Soviet government did not condone such acts, little was done to stop them.

Stalin's attitude stemmed in part from his own anti-semitism rein-forced by the fact that many of his party enemies, real or imagined, were or had been Jews, but it also had a sound political basis. German propa-ganda had proclaimed the invasion of the Soviet Union to be a war

111

against Jewish Bolshevism; Stalin did not intend to play into the German hands by acknowledging in any way even the slightest connection between his government and the Jews. In large measure, this same attitude still prevails in the present day Soviet Union: the *Great Soviet Encyclopaedia* article on Auschwitz lists the victims by nationality and thus Jews are not included. This is in a sense correct, but it also neatly obscures the real meaning of Auschwitz.

The Germans

Although some Germans were surely deeply moved by the incontrovertible evidence of the evil of the regime underscored by the liberation of the camps, the more normal response, according to eyewitnesses, was a combination of indifference, denial and self-excuses. As Ritchie Calder said, in 1945 the German people lacked the moral acceptance of defeat and were "neither humble nor contrite." Only a tiny fraction were willing to admit the concept of collective guilt, a doctrine proclaimed interestingly enough by *Das Schwarze Korps* in which an editorial on February 1, 1945, stated baldly that "there are no innocents in Germany."

The Allied military commanders, in an effort to counter the commonly heard view that "these things did not really happen," forced German civilians in the vicinity of the camps to visit them and in some cases to help bury the dead. Others local commanders made attendance at movies showing the camps at the time of liberation mandatory. In the British sector at such a showing two young girls laughed during the performance and were summarily ordered to view the film a second time. But these efforts had at most a short-term impact on a few people; most seemed to be little affected.

The Nuremberg trials documented in overwhelming detail the whole story of genocide but had little impact on the German people. The condemned were for the most part believed to be victims of victors' justice and no more. There was even a rumor that the bodies in the camps were in fact victims of a far-off plague who had been shipped to Germany in refrigerator ships. Many Germans complained privately about the behavior of the Jewish survivors claiming that most were blackmarketeers (as some no doubt were), as though the venial misdeeds of a few Jews in the camps balanced the scales of justice.

Great resentment was aroused by rumors that the Jews might demand and receive their property back as though such a demand was just another injustice heaped upon the long-suffering German people. Interestingly enough, after the defeat, a remarkable number of Germans claimed Jewish ancestors hoping that in this way they would gain a kind of protective coloration against suspicions and accusations.

112

But it would be a mistake to read too much into the lack of German feelings of guilt because in the rubble years virtually all the psychological and physical energy of the German population was consumed in the mere struggle for survival. A few scholars, a few religious men, some emigrés might concern themselves with dissecting the national soul but to the average man such idle speculation was a luxury he could ill-afford. By 1948–49 a few were beginning to come to grips with the moral dimensions of the German problem, but as Günter G. Grass ruefully noted, the *Wirtschaftwunder* (economic miracle) submerged such somber thoughts in a rising tide of prosperity.

Jewish Attitudes

At the moment of liberation the 11 million Jews in the world could be divided into four overlapping groups. First and foremost were the camp survivors, only a tiny fragment of the world Jewish community, but who despite their small numbers had a place in the moral universe quite unlike any other human beings. Primo Levi wrote that the survivors of the camps can never truly forget and indeed should not do so, for they have a moral obligation to those who died. "We must be listened to above and beyond our personal experiences, we have collectively been witnesses of a fundamental, unexpected event, fundamental precisely because unexpected, not forseen by anyone. . . .It happened, therefore it can happen again; that is the core of what we have to say."[7] That handful who had seen things no other humans had seen, who had experienced things beyond the power of imagination of the normal man were bound to ask, "How did it happen? Why did I survive? Who was responsible?" The survivors also pondered the future asking themselves, "Who am I? Where should I go? What is my future?" and above all "What is a Jew?" The answers of the survivors to these questions were to have a special moral force.

The second group is what might be called the "free survivors," those million or more Jews who lived in National Socialist dominated Europe but were never sent to the camps. These free survivors had lived anxiety-filled lives; fear had been their constant companion, but in comparison to the camp survivors they were for the most part physically and mentally unimpaired. A few even attempted to resume their former lives; this is particularly true of those who lived in fully assimilated communities, like the French Jews or the Italian Jews. Many, however, who survived in countries with high levels of anti-semitism in the best of times were ready recruits for settlement in Palestine. Most of the Jews from Poland, Hungary, Rumania and the Baltic states passionately sought to leave Europe as soon as possible.

Third, there were those European Jews who were citizens of the victorious states—the Russians and the English. They had lived out the war in comparative safety—speaking of course, of those Russian Jews who resided in areas beyond the high water mark of German advance or who had escaped to the East ahead of the advancing Germans. These Jews felt a loyalty to their homeland, and though they were no doubt deeply sympathetic with their brethren in the camps did not feel akin to them. In 1945 they had little interest in emigrating to Palestine. True, as the years went by the Soviet Jews became increasingly disenchanted with their regime and its attitude toward them, but in the glow of victory Soviet Jews appeared to feel a surge of patriotism not much different from their gentile neighbors.

Finally, there were the American Jews, in 1945 almost one-third of the world community. They gave generously to relief organizations; lobbied the government to act on behalf of the survivors; lent their names, prestige and purses to organizations dedicated to helping the victims. But most also went out of their way to emphasize that they were Americans first. The cause of the victims was not in any direct way their cause. They felt warm, human sympathy but not political kinship with the European Jews. They emphasized repeatedly that their interest in the fate of the survivors was not to be construed as evidence that they in some mystical sense considered themselves Jews first and Americans second. There is virtually no evidence in the American Jewish publications of the immediate postwar period that the American Jews blamed the American government, its "good and great president" and its "valiant army" for not doing everything that could be done to save as many Jews as could be saved from the murderous wrath of the Nazis.

Interestingly enough, the Jews in all four categories tended to blame themselves in some degree for the Holocaust. The camp survivors themselves were often haunted by vague feelings of guilt: "I felt innocent, yes, but enrolled among the saved and therefore in permanent search of a justification in my own eyes and those of others." And those in safe havens also wondered if they personally or their communities collectively had done everything that could have been done to save the victims. This guilt was not pervasive and it would be a mistake to exaggerate it; but it is important to underscore the fact that the Jews in the years immediately after the war were more inclined to take on some share of the responsibility themselves.

Actions

Thus far we have considered, for the most part, the change in attitudes brought on by the liberation. Undoubtedly the anti-semitism of the National Socialist regime from 1933 on had some impact on popular attitudes from the start, but it was the images of the liberated camps and the harrowing accounts of the survivors that made anti-semitism socially unacceptable to an ever-widening segment of the Western population. And these new attitudes made possible policy decisions which only months before would have seemed politically risky.

In the summer of 1945 President Truman sent Earl Harrison, a former Commissioner of Emigration, to inquire into the conditions and needs of the Displaced Persons, which in effect meant the needs and conditions of the Jews remaining in the camps because most other DPs had already been repatriated. On September 29, 1945, Harrison's report to the President was made public. It was a stinging indictment. "As matters now stand we appear to be treating the Jews as the Nazis treated them except that we do not exterminate them."[8] Even conceding the often staggering ineptitude of the American Army of Occupation in its treatment of the Jews, this statement betrays an utter inability to comprehend even on the most rudimentary level the nature and purposes of the Nazi regime. Harrison cited as evidence for his charge the existence of barbed wire fences (true), armed guards (true) and prohibitions from leaving the camps without a pass (true). He also noted that the camps were often unsanitary and overcrowded and a standard ration was only 2,000 calories a day (all true). But to suggest that these conditions bear any conceivable comparison to the Nazi camps is grotesque.

For the short term Harrison recommended improved rations, more sympathetic officers, and the use of qualified Jews rather than Germans in military offices. These measures, however, were only palliatives. For the long term Harrison recommended that those Jews well enough to travel be removed from Germany and admitted to the United States or other countries of their choice under existing immigration laws. For those still too weak to travel, he recommended transfer from the camps to nursing homes. In September 1945 his long-term solution was feasible. If the highest figure of camp survivors is taken— 100,000—perhaps one-third wished to return to their former homes (especially French, Czechoslovaks, rather surprisingly Rumanians and even some Poles) and one-third were probably in need of long-term hospitalization. The remaining one-third—say 30,000—could without any significant change in the laws have been allowed to emigrate to the United States. But what was true in September was no longer true in early 1946 when the numbers in the camps, rather than dimishing, began growing as an increasing number of free Jews, those who had never been in Hitler's camps, voluntarily entered the American camps.

As for Harrison's short-term recommendations, they were implemented rapidly with Eisenhower himself overseeing the operation. Every DP was allotted 30 square feet, the same as assigned to American soldiers; in most cases Jews were removed from the old camps to better accommodations; and calories per day were increased to 2,500.

What is most suggestive about the Harrison report is that it cast the United States Army in the role of unwitting "oppressor" of the Jews, and that this charge not only did not raise any political storm, it was accepted quite calmly, and the recommendations made in the report were implemented more or less as a matter of course. Jews were singled out for "special treatment," and the American government acted as if this was perfectly reasonable; the American people accordingly raised no objection. It is hard to believe that in an analogous situation in, say, 1939 the response would have been the same.

The British government was faced with a much more complex problem, namely Palestine. To allow free immigration as the Zionists demanded would lead to a flood of refugees and an unquestionably violent Arab reaction. Despite the fact that the government of Great Britain was socialist and that party had long supported Zionism, the Prime Minister Clement Attlee was adamant in not capitulating to extreme Zionist demands. He was even unwilling to go as far as the recommendations of an Anglo-American Committee published in a White Paper of May 1946 which called for a continuation of the Mandate "until hostility between Arab and Jews disappears;" the admission of 100,000 victims of persecution; the suppression of violence; and finally and most significantly "ensuring the rights and position of the other sections of the population were not prejudiced."

Attlee's first act after the publication of the White Paper was the arrest of a number of members of the Jewish Agency because they were members of the Haganah, the Jewish underground army which had been involved in violence. In defending the government repression a spokesman stated: "The Government must ... resist the wave of terrorism and approach the whole problem on a much broader basis, and not force on the Arabs the responsibility for taking large numbers of immigrants from Central Europe, but to make other countries responsible, this country and America, to play their part."[9] During the next months there followed a rising cycle of violence which included the blowing-up of the King David Hotel on July 22, 1946, and the execution of three British sergeants by Jewish terrorists.

At the end of 1946, 18 months after the end of the war, the refugee problem remained unsolved with no solution likely in the forseeable future. If the British were determined to maintain the Mandate until tranquillity was restored and at the same time severely restrict the immigration of Jews from Europe, Palestine would remain for the indefinite future an unlikely home for the surviving remnant. And with little chance that American immigration laws would be dramatically altered the possibility of large scale re-settlement of Jews in the United States was also precluded. Europe also offered, at best, bleak prospects. Germany was too impoverished to provide more than temporary shelter in Allied-run camps; Western nations were willing to welcome their nationals back but had no interest or capacity in taking on the homeless Jews in the camps.

The establishment of the Polish Provisional Government on June 28, 1945—the first government in Polish history actively opposed to anti-Semitism—created a flurry of hope. This hope was buttressed by the government's statement that it would welcome the return of 250,000 Polish Jews who had survived in the Soviet Union. In the autumn of 1945 some of the Polish Jews in German camps decided to make their way back to their homeland which now gave every indication of wanting them to return. But the Polish government, whatever its real attitude might have been, was unable or unwilling to curb the ensuing violent anti-Semitic outbursts. In the course of 1945 over 400 Jews were murdered. The majority of the camp survivors who had gone to Poland in 1945 made their way back to the West by the end of the year and were joined by a growing stream of Jews who had been repatriated by the Soviet Union also going to the West.

The first reaction of the British and Americans was to block these Jews at the border, but in the end the Allies simply did not have the heart to turn the pitiful stream of refugees back. The net result was that throughout 1946 the numbers of Jews in the camps in the West grew dramatically. For every Jew who left the camps at least two new refugees arrived.

Liberation convinced the people of the West that the Jews—as the special victims of the National Socialists, as those who had suffered the most—deserved special treatment. Before liberation special treatment was considered politically dangerous and likely to rouse latent anti-semitism; after liberation it had become politically acceptable. But there was a yawning gap between the abstract idea of special treatment and the actions necessary to make it a reality. Truman was perfectly willing to see that the conditions in the camps were dramatically improved, but he was not willing to ask Congress to allow the survivors to enter the United States. The British, too, improved conditions in their camps, but they balked at allowing more than a handful of Jews into Palestine. In time, of course, pressures from Jews and Gentiles alike, as well as a sense of justice, forced both the British and the Americans to change their positions. With the almost simultaneous creation of Israel and a change in the American immigration laws in 1948 the entire refugee problem evaporated in a matter of months.

Liberation had a profound impact on public opinion in the West not because of what it revealed about genocide, but because of what the average person thought it revealed. First in the popular mind, the liberation confirmed the "fact" of genocide. As one contemporary put it: "To the world at large, the overshadowing event after the collapse of the Nazi regime was the liberation of the concentration camps and the huge army of slave laborers in Germany." As the camps were being liberated

Churchill himself spoke of the "dire sink of iniquity," but if Bergen-Belsen, Dachau and the rest deserved such a telling phrase, the English language would break down in trying to describe Treblinka and Auschwitz.

Secondly, liberation tended to focus the moral indignation of the West on the Germans—the account of the liberation of Bergen-Belsen "shocked the British public beyond measure and raised to a white heat its indignation against the Nazi regime and even against the German people in general." Stalin, whose crimes were in every way as great as Hitler's, did not share equivalent reprobation—his camps had not been thrown open to public inspection.

Third, liberation provided an overwhelming moral justification for the war, so no embarassing questions were raised about the Allied conduct of the war, in particular British terror bombing. The Germans had, in the eyes of the world, lost all rights to blame anyone for anything.

Liberation futhermore dealt a powerful blow to anti-semitism in the West. It was routinely predicted that anti-semitism would get a new lease on life once the war ended. George Orwell, writing in *Commentary* in 1945, reported that anti-semitism in England was on the increase because in the eyes of the ordinary Englishman, the Jews were the people who benefited the most from the war. And yet anti-semitism rather than being exacerbated after the war tended to diminish dramatically. The American film industry, timid to the point of cowardice when it came to dealing with social issues which might offend any segment of the audience, actually began to make movies like *Gentleman's Agreement,* which were frankly pro-semitic. Furthermore, American movie distributors refused to touch David Lean's *Oliver Twist* because it might be interpreted as anti-semitic.

It would be a mistake to read too much into the liberation of the camps. The shaping of the postwar world was the product of many forces, many decisions, many personalities, and liberation was only one—rather small—factor, but it did play a role that was not without consequences.

1. The most "scholarly" work is by Wilhelm Stäglich, *Der Auschwitz-Mythos* (Tübingen, 1979).
2. Arthur Morse, *While Six Million Died* (New York, 1967). Morse is a serious author and I do not imply that he should in any way be linked with Stäglich. However, the very title of his book implies that the policy of genocide was initiated before the outbreak of the war. That is surely debatable.
3. *New York Times,* August 16, 1945.
4. See Martin Gilbert, *Auschwitz and the Allies* (New York, 1981).
5. David Wyman, "Why Auschwitz was Never Bombed." *Commentary* (May

1978). See also a letter by Milt Groban in *Commentary* (July 1978). Groban was a Radar Navigator-Bombadier in the 15th Air Force. His refutation of Wyman's argument is crushing.

6. Elliot Cohen, "An Act of Affirmation." *Commentary* (November 1945).
7. Primo Levi, *The Drowned and the Saved* (London, 1988).
8. The *New York Times* (September 30, 1945) has the entire Harrison Report.
9. See *Hansard,* July 1, 1946, pp. 1795–1798.

APPENDICES

The following three accounts of liberation are given in full both because of their literary merit and the reliability of the witnesses.

APPENDIX A

Clara Greenbaum's Account of the Liberation of Bergen-Belsen

The last day began just like all the others had. From the very begining, I had made a point of inventing all sorts of little rituals and procedures for myself—to give me something to hang on to, if you know what I mean. So each morning I would wake up by myself a few minutes before the *Block Kapo* [the trustee prisoner in charge of the barrack] came in. The first thing I would do was to check that my children were all right. I was the *de facto* nanny of our *Block*. If a child's mother died, or if there were too many women to allow a mother and child to share a bunk, the children would be moved to the bunk behind me, where my own children slept. Sometimes—it depended on how long a child stayed alive—there would be as many as five in that bunk.

Ordinarily I would wake them up so that they wouldn't be frightened out of their sleep by the *Kapo's* shouts and curses when he came in. But sometimes they looked so angelic in their sleep that I just couldn't bear to wake them up and force them back into this terrible world in which we were living. It was selfish of me, I know, and I would feel guilty about this afterward, when they were woken up so brutally by the *Kapo* and I would have to comfort them.

But today was such a day. I let them sleep. Anyway, the next thing I would do every morning was to see whether the two women in my bunk were alive. If they were, good for them. But if they were dead, I wanted to be the first to know it. Every prisoner had some little treasures hidden away in her clothes—a small scrap of food, or something—and so I would try always to be the first to search a corpse for that. Also, if you needed an extra pair of socks, or a scarf, whatever, just about your only chance of getting it was from a dead body.

This day, both women were alive. Having made this little inspection, I lay back again and updated my calendar. It wasn't a written calendar, or anything like that, and I never really knew what day of the week it was for sure, or the date. What I counted was the number of days I had been in the camp. I just kept the figure in my head, and would update it every morning, first thing. During the course of the day I would repeat the number to myself so that I wouldn't get it wrong. I'm amazed that this system was entirely accurate. When I got out of the camp, one of the first things I did was to check my number against a calendar. It was right on the nose: eight hundred and eighteen days!

123

Then I always had another few moments before the *Kapo* came. Those were the best moments of the day for me. I was awake, almost no one else was, it was quiet and peaceful, and I felt that I had some semblance of privacy. Oddly enough, that was one of the things I missed most in the camp. Not food or anything like that, though of course I missed those, but privacy. You could never be by yourself.

So I lay back, my head resting on my hands, and enjoyed the luxury of the moment—the luxury of being oblivious to other people, sounds, thoughts, feelings. . . .

The next thing I knew, I was waking up again! I had fallen asleep! This had never happened to me before, and I was in a terrible panic. For a second I thought I must be dead, because there seemed no other way of accounting for the fact that I hadn't been woken by the *Kapo*. And then an even worse panic. I must have missed the morning *Appell,* the roll call. The punishments for that were terrible. In fact, in our camp you could be hanged for less. I looked for my children. They were still sleeping. I thought, Oh, my God. They, too, are going to be punished. . . .

And then I realized that I was not alone. In fact, no one had left the room, even though, as I could soon tell, most people were awake. Some women were standing in the aisle between the bunks; just standing there, not walking. Some were sitting on the edges of the lowest tier of bunks. A few were whispering to each other. Everything I saw and felt told me that something terrible had happened. The *Kapo* had not come in to wake us up!

You must understand. In that world, when something went wrong, it was something which had gone wrong for the prisoners and would bring some new torture, some new indignity, to us. Not to one of the guards, of course. Their destiny was infinitely above us, so much so that they were like gods. Really, they *were* our gods, since everything in our lives, just about, and certainly our lives, seemed to be at their whim.

And so when we weren't woken up, there could be only one explanation. They were playing some fiendish new game with us, like a cat does with a mouse that is in its power. What kind of game? Who could tell. Perhaps they did not wake us up so that we would all miss the *Appell,* and then all of us would be punished for having missed it.

We stayed in the *Block* for a long time. I've no idea how long, perhaps it was two or three hours. Certainly they were the longest hours in my life. No, I didn't think anything. My mind was completely blank; you see, I was so utterly frightened. Every second might be the one in which the doors would suddenly be kicked open, with guards and dogs and guns firing. I was quite rigid with fear; my fists were clenched. Goodness only knows how fast my heart was beating. And you couldn't hear a sound.

Suddenly there was a horrible scream, which almost made me die with fright. This is it, I told myself, and I turned around for my children. Can you imagine: the poor babies, they were also awake and were lying petrified like the rest of us! But it wasn't the guards. One of the women had gone crazy and was running toward the door, stumbling over other women, colliding with the posts that held up the roof. For a short moment, as she opened the door, the room was filled with light, and then she slammed it behind her and was gone, though we could still hear her screams, growing fainter every moment.

We all knew that in the next second a shot would ring out: a guard would have had his morning target practice. In fact, there was no sound, and in a while we could no longer hear the woman. But that didn't mean anything, of course.

Now the silence in the barracks was, if anything, even more complete. If you can imagine being even more frightened than utterly and totally frightened, that's how I was feeling now.

After some time—again I can't tell you how long it was—there was again a sudden flood of light, but this time without any noise. I came to my sense sufficiently to realize that one of the women had crept out of the building to see what was going on.

But she, too, did not come back. And once again the complete terror, the complete silence.

And a third time the door opened. Another woman, as silently as the one before, had gone out to see what was happening.

This one, though, left the door open behind her, and it was as if the light that now filled the room also cleared my head a little. I was still horribly frightened, but I noticed that I was also very thirsty. From my childhood—oh, God, how far away that was!—I remembered the doves Noah sent out. The first two did not return, but the third did. But I put that out of my head as quickly as I could. In the concentration camp you cannot have hope. Only determination.

Presently I could hear some soft noises, as if there was some movement going on near the door. I lifted myself up on one elbow, and because we were on the third tier, I had a good view, even though we were at the far end of the room. I could see that a lot of women had gathered by the door and that some of them were taking that brave, dangerous step into the outside.

Hannah and Adam, my two children, climbed over and lay next to me, their faces buried into my body. I could feel how heavily they were breathing. You know, this was the first time in two years that they had come to me in my bunk. Once, at the very beginning, they had tried to, but the women in my bunk screamed at them that there was no room, and they never tried that again. I'll never forget how, that time, after she finished screaming at the children, one of the women muttered to herself, but audibly, "What the hell are kids doing in this place, anyway?"

But now the women didn't object. They knew, as everyone did by now, that something special was going on. Soon, most of the bunks between us and the door had been emptied. I climbed down, and the children did the same. It wasn't a question of deciding to climb down. You did what everyone else did in the camp as a matter of course. There were hardly any matters on which you decided yourself.

Hannah and Adam each held one of my hands; the other children were close behind. We walked to the door. I should say that my mind was still quite blank, that I was still horribly frightened. But I remember that all the bunks we passed were empty. This was unusual. Ordinarily, when we got up in the morning for *Appell,* there were always at least eight or nine people who didn't get up. They were dead, or just about dead. Or else, even if they still had strength in their bones, they had lost their will to live, and just would not get up. Sometimes we talked to them, tried to revive some desire in them to live, but at other times we had no help to give them, and they would be shot.

We were outside. It was a pleasant day, slightly overcast, but bright. Again I felt an awful thirst, and I thought that I would stop at a certain place near the *Appellplatz,* the assembly ground, where there was a ditch, and see if I could get some water there, since it had rained the previous night.

I was in luck. Not too many people knew of this place since it was just underneath the overhang of a building—between the piers on which the building stood, I should say—and although the water was muddy, it was fresh.

We moved to the *Appellplatz.* For the first time, I became aware of hundreds, thousands of other people. From all sides they were converging on the *Appellplatz.* Many were walking by themselves, but there were also some who were leaning on friends or relatives, and others who were crawling on all fours, too weak to walk. Some of these had collapsed before reaching the *Appellplatz* and just lay on the ground, dying. You didn't stop to pick them up—what was the use?—and I didn't think too much about it then. But I often think about them now, the people who died on that last day, and I wish that I had stopped at least once to help one of them, if only by saying a few comforting words to them.

The first thing that struck me when we were on the *Appellplatz* was that prisoners were standing or sitting or lying all over the square in an entirely disorderly way. I had never seen that before. Ordinarily, the *Appellplatz* was a place to avoid, since it was completely open, and just that fact made you feel insecure—you felt exposed there. But it wasn't only that. It was, objectively, a dangerous place because it was where the particularly sadistic guards would hang around when they were bored. They would wait until a prisoner who for some reason had to cross the *Appellplatz*—perhaps someone who did not have the strength to walk around it, or who simply didn't know better—appeared, and then they would find some way of amusing themselves with her. So the only times one would go to the *Appellplatz* was for morning or evening roll calls, or when they made us all turn out to watch a hanging, which wasn't always during the regular *Appell*. Of all the places in the camp, I hated that spot the most.

This was the first time I had seen the *Appellplatz* looking so *untidy*, and that bothered me. It's almost as if I wanted there to be carefully drawn up lines of prisoners, rather than people just scattered all over the place. I can't tell you how disorienting that was, and of course it only increased my anxiety.

I had already noticed by this time that there were no guards around. I'd even looked up at the guard towers and seen that they were empty. You might think that this would have astonished me and delighted me. But it didn't. I'd noticed that the guards had disappeared and thought no more about it.

How can I explain this? Somehow, deep inside me, I had always known that I was going to survive, and that one day I would be liberated. You can put this down to wishful thinking, but the fact is that I always, always was completely certain of this. Which is not to say that I didn't also have many moments when I thought I was about to be killed. Nowadays I tend to think that the main thing that gave me this confidence was that I knew my children would not survive without me. Hannah was seven, and Adam just under four. There was no way I was going to let them die.

But today didn't seem like the day of liberation, because I was much too frightened. The fact that the guards had disappeared did not seem to me to mean anything more than they had disappeared. It was almost incidental to the entire situation. One reason for this, I'm sure, is that we were very much less organized than most camps, where prisoners had ways of learning about what was going on in the outside world and so on. We had none of that, no real way of knowing how the war was going, or that the Allies were close at hand.

But apart from that, there was never a moment in the camp when you weren't aware of the guards. During the day, you saw them everywhere, but even if there were periods when there were no guards in sight, you had their image printed on your retina, and you could not escape them. At night you dreamed about them. They were, in that horrible sense I described earlier, our gods, and we were like primitive savages who are votaries of a fearsome and evil deity. So the fact that the guards weren't visible today did not mean that they were not there. They were. In our minds. And believe me, for many people they still are there to this day.

Perhaps this will help you understand what I'm saying. We were on the *Appellplatz* for a very long time. I'm sure it must have been at least four hours. During that time, so far as I'm aware, all of us stayed *on* the

Appellplatz. No one approached the gates, or even the firing line—the line near the fence where any prisoner would be shot on sight. Isn't that odd? Today we could have walked to the firing line without danger, for there were no guards on the towers. In fact, we could have walked to the gates, opened them, and simply left the camp. Physically, a number of us had sufficient strength to manage all that. But the fact is that we didn't, because the guards were *inside* us. To such an extent, we had become slaves.

What were my thoughts during this time? I hardly had any, to tell you the truth. The main thing is that I was overwhelmingly anxious. And that also has to do with being a slave. You see, we were now in a sense free, because the guards weren't there. Part of me thought that they might return at any moment, doing horrible things to us; but another part of me slowly began to realize that they had left, that this was all over—one way or another.

Can you imagine, in any way, how terrifying this freedom was to us? There was so little in our lives. Almost everything we had, the structure of our lives, came from the guards. In some ways it was irrelevant to us how brutal they were. In fact, their very brutality pointed up their power, their command of the situation, and in a perverted way reassured us, who had absolutely no power, no control over our lives, that the world had not disintegrated *completely.* Think of the savages with their evil god. They hate their god and are desperately frightened of him. But what happens when that god vanishes, taking with him every last semblance of structure that is left in their lives? Taking away the purpose of their lives, almost, which has up to now been primarily to confirm the god's divine nature?

I know this sounds sick to you. But did you suppose for a moment that it was only our bodies that were imprisoned—and tortured?

So I stood there on the *Appellplatz* for hour after hour. I was like a zombie, mentally and physically immobile. Adam stood with me, holding my hand still. Hannah and the two orphans sat close by me. They were too weak to stand, though none of them was seriously ill.

Just beyond the wire fence, on the north side, there were some fields, which were plowed and cultivated all the time we were there. An old farmer, I remember, and a horse which looked even older than he. Quite often, I used to take the children to where we could look at those fields. I wanted them to see crops grow, and to see an animal other than the big dogs that the guards had. And sometimes I used to point toward the fields and the world outside, and I would say *"Freiheit,"* freedom. It was one of the first words Adam learned; I planned it that way.

Just behind the fields there were some hills. They were low hills, with scrub growing on them and one or two trees. Today, when we were standing on the *Appellplatz,* we faced in the direction of these fields and hills.

Hours went by in more or less complete silence. But then I heard a noise. It was a metallic, clanking noise—not at all unpleasant, though at first it wasn't very loud—and it seemed to be coming from behind the hilltop.

Just about everyone else heard the sound, too, and people began perking up. In a moment I saw something move. At first I could not make out what it was. All I could see was a long, thin rod, as it seemed to be, pointing up to the sky; and I remember wondering how that rod fitted the sound we were hearing.

Then the rod tilted down a bit, and I could see that it was in fact the gun barrel of a tank. For a few moments I could not see or hear anything more because of the commotion on the *Appellplatz*.

So, then, this really was the end. They were going to mow us down with their machine guns. Or perhaps they were going to drive over us, crushing our bodies under the tracks of their tanks.

As people do in such situations, we all huddled close together. I gave Hannah my hand, pulled her to her feet. The two orphans managed to get to their feet, too, and then the five of us joined in the rush—well, it was hardly a rush, no one had the strength for that, but you know what I mean—to the center of the *Appellplatz*.

All this was taking place perhaps thirty or forty yards away from me, so I could see quite well. The troops climbed down from their trucks; all the tank hatches were opened, and more soldiers, wearing funny helmets, climbed down from the tanks.

There were no orders given—I know that because I could have heard. As a group, but a rather disorderly one—they weren't in any kind of military formation—the soldiers came up to the wire. One of them threw something at the fence—I suppose to see whether it was electrified—and when they saw it wasn't they came up closer still. I would say that there were as many as four or five hundred men. I remember noticing that they didn't appear particularly different from Germans. I don't know what I expected them to look like.

They came up to the fence, as I say, and just stood there looking at us. I couldn't understand their behavior at all. I thought about that; in fact, it had suddenly become very important to me to try to figure out why they were just standing there and staring at us. But I couldn't make any sense of that. I wish I could tell you how eerie that was, watching them staring at us in that inexplicable way.

But then I saw one of the soldiers double over and throw up. Soon another was doing the same, and then another. And then I understood. They were looking at us in disgust. We repelled them. We made them feel like vomiting!

A deep despair came over me. I felt like Adam when he first knew he was naked: horribly and irremediably ashamed. I looked around me and saw myself and the other prisoners for the first time through the eyes of those British soldiers. We were disgusting to look at, no doubt about it. It's odd, isn't it, that I had never really realized that before.

A moment after that first soldier threw up, a strange thing happened among the prisoners. We began turning away from them. We turned our backs to them. We didn't want them to see us. And if, a short while before, we had in some dim kind of way wanted them to come into the camp, now, very strongly, we wanted them to stay where they were—or else to go away. We were so ashamed of ourselves.

Our movement triggered off something among the soldiers. Some of them, at one end of the crowd, began throwing things over the fence, and from the scrambling among the prisoners I assumed it was food. The soldiers nearest the gate, however, formed into some kind of rank and stood at attention. I saw that one of the soldiers in the strange helmets had climbed into a tank. He started up its engine and then rammed through the camp gate. When it was down, he backed over it, crushing it into little fragments, and then parked the tank in its former spot.

We might all have gotten ourselves killed in the crush if the panic had lasted for more than a few moments. But then, at the same instant almost, people throughout the crowd noticed that the second tank, immediately behind the first one, was flying a Union Jack—the British flag—from its turret.

We moved back a step or two. Those who had been sitting down before the first tank appeared sat down again. Motionless, once more, and in complete silence, we watched.

More and more tanks followed. I don't remember how many there were, but there were a lot of them. And behind them were trucks, military trucks, with their canvas tops down so we could see the soldiers sitting on benches.

The first tank came up to the main gate and then stopped. The rest of the convoy halted behind it. Then the hatch on top of the front tank opened and a man stuck his head out of it. He did not move and seemed just to stare in our direction.

Then the tank began moving off to the side, stopped for a moment, and then started up again, creeping slowly past the fence of the camp. The other vehicles followed. None of the other tanks opened their hatches, but in the trucks all the soldiers had got to their feet, holding onto the rails above their heads, and were looking in our direction.

The entire convoy began circling the camp. A while later—it may have been about 20 minutes, because they weren't moving very fast— the first tank reached the main gate again. It stopped. The man was still looking out of the turret hatch. The entire convoy stopped behind the front tank. And then, a moment later, the front tank began moving again.

All this time I had been feeling completely blank, but now I was seized by the fear that the British were going to leave us. A moment later, through, I saw that that wasn't the case, and I felt relieved. The British were not leaving. They were circling the camp for a second time! It was one of the strangest things I've ever seen. Certainly it was one of the strangest things of that day.

So they went around a second time, and when they had done that, they drew up in a near formation in front of the gates. First the tanks, then the trucks turned off their motors. It was again completely quiet.

By now all the other soldiers had formed into ranks and, at an officer's command, marched into the camp. We were liberated.

Do you think that that really meant very much to me? Sure, in some distant way it did, but only in a very distant way. I took my children by the hand and walked away from the soldiers, who suddenly had become very busy and purposeful. I had no idea what they were going to do—what does one do when one liberates a concentration camp?—and all I knew was that I didn't want to have any of them look at me in that way again. I wanted to walk off and hide behind one of the barracks.

It was Hannah who wouldn't let me. I took a few steps away from the soldiers when I heard a sound that was terrible, but which I could not at first identify, even though in some strange and remote way it seemed familiar to me. Then I understood. My daughter was crying. She was crying! Do you understand? For the first time in three years this little child was crying! She was crying so hard that I thought her thin little body would collapse under the force of its convulsions.

She had known that you cannot allow your feelings in the concentration camp. But she also knew, now, that she could cry, that it was safe to cry.

And she was crying for her father, the father she had last seen when she was four years old and could scarcely remember. I tell you, I have never in my life heard any cry of pain like that child's. Adam, too, was crying, but he was crying like a small child, as he had done a few times before in the camp, and I don't think he really had a sense of what was going on. But Hannah's cry was different. It was the most tragic wail I have known. If it was like anything, it was like the mourning of an old woman.

And I? I followed my daughter's example; I learned from her. I sat down with her, and for several minutes I screamed. Oh, I screamed so loudly. I can't tell you exactly why I did it, but I had to so badly, and while I screamed I pounded my fists into the ground, and finally I collapsed sobbing, lying on the ground with my face down.

I felt strong hands lift up my shoulders and bring me to my feet. I was hardly aware of it, I was still sobbing so much. But the touch of those hands opened up something else in me, and I knew that what I wanted more than anything else in the world was for someone to put his arms around me, and hold me, and rock me slightly while I cried on his chest. And that's what he did, and what I did, and after a while I realized that like little Hannah I, too, was screaming for my father.

All this time the soldier was holding me, and my head was buried in his chest, not only because I wanted it to be there but also because I couldn't bear the thought of him looking at me with that look of disgust. And when I stopped crying I turned away from him so that he couldn't see me, and took my children, and walked off. I've often wondered who that soldier was, what he looked like.

The British were slowly getting the camp organized. There was a huge table set up, and soldiers were dishing out soup for us. But when we got to the table I realized that the soup was too rich, and I asked for some water, with which I diluted it. But even then it was more than our stomachs could bear, and it made us feel a bit sick. But other prisoners, who had gulped the soup down without diluting it, were in much worse shape, and I think that some even died from it.

The rest of the day passed by quickly enough. I was exhausted, the children even more so, but the British would not let us go to sleep until after a short interrogation in which they asked for our names, names of relatives, that kind of thing, for a Red Cross list. That night I slept in a bunk alone with my two children. And that was the end of my last day as a prisoner.

APPENDIX B

Simon Wiesenthal's Account of the Liberation
of Mauthausen

It was ten o'clock on the morning of May 5, 1945, when I saw a big gray tank with a white star on its side and the American flag waving from the turret. I stood on the windswept square that had been, until an hour earlier, the courtyard of the Mauthausen concentration camp. The day was sunny, with a scent of spring in the air. Gone was the sweetish smell of burned flesh that had always hovered over the yard.

The night before, the last SS men had run away. The machinery of death had come to a stop. In my room, a few dead people were lying on their bunks. They hadn't been taken away this morning. The crematorium no longer operated.

I do not remember how I'd got from my room into the courtyard. I was hardly able to walk. I was wearing my faded striped uniform with a yellow J in a yellow-red double triangle. Around me I saw other men in striped dungarees. Some were holding small flags, waving at the Americans. Where had they gotten the flags from? Did the Americans bring them? I shall never know.

The tank with the white star was about a hundred yards in front of me. I wanted to touch the star, but I was too weak. I had survived to see this day, but I couldn't make the last hundred yards. I remember taking a few steps, and then my knees gave way and I fell on my face.

Somebody lifted me up. I felt the rough texture of an olive-drab, American uniform brush against my bare arms. I couldn't speak; I couldn't even open my mouth. I pointed toward the white star, I touched the cold, dusty armor with my hands, and then I fainted.

When I opened my eyes after what seemed a long time, I was back on my bunk. The room seemed changed. There was only one man on each bunk, no longer three or four, and the dead had been taken away. There was an unfamiliar smell in the air. It was DDT. They brought in big kettles with soup. This was real soup, and it tasted delicious. I took too much of it—my stomach wasn't used to such nourishing fare—and I got violently sick.

The next days went by in a pleasant apathy. Most of the time I dozed on my bunk. American doctors in white coats came to look at us. We were given pills and more food—soup, vegetables, meat. I still was so weak that a friend had to help me when I wanted to go out. I had survived, I didn't have to force myself to be strong any longer; I had seen the day I'd prayed for all these years, but now I was weaker than ever. "A natural reaction," said the doctors.

I made an effort to get up and walk out alone. As I shuffled through a dark corridor, a man jumped at me and knocked me down. I collapsed and lost consciousness. I came to on my bunk, and an American doctor gave me something. Two friends sat next to me. They had picked me up in the corridor and carried me to my bunk. They said that a Polish trustee had beaten me. Perhaps he was angry because I was still alive.

People in room A said I must report the trustee to the American authorities. We were free men now, no longer *Untermenschen* (subhumans). The next day my friends accompanied me to an office in the building that had formerly been the camp headquarters. A handwritten sign WAR CRIMES was on the door. We were told to wait in a small anteroom. Somebody brought me a chair, and I sat down.

Through the open doors, I saw American officers behind desks who interrogated SS men who stood at attention in front of them. Several former prisoners worked as typists. An SS man was brought into the room. Instinctively, I turned my head sideward so he wouldn't see me. He had been a brutal guard, when he walked through the corridor and a prisoner did not step aside quickly and snap to attention, the SS man would whip the prisoner's face with the riding crop he always carried. The sight of this man had always brought cold sweat to the back of my neck.

Now I stared, I couldn't believe it. The SS man was trembling, just as we had trembled before him. His shoulders were hunched, and I noticed that he wiped the palms of his hands. He was no longer a superman, he made me think of a trapped animal. He was escorted by a Jewish prisoner—a former prisoner.

I kept staring, fascinated. I didn't hear what was said as the SS man stood before the American interrogator. He could hardly stand at attention, and there was sweat on his forehead. The American officer motioned with his hand and an American soldier took the SS man away. My friends said that all SS men were being taken to a big concrete pillbox, where they were to be kept under guard until they were tried. I made my report on the Polish trustee. My friends testified that they had found me lying unconscious in the corridor. One of the American doctors also testified. Then we went back to our room. That night the trustee apologized to me in front of our comrades, and extended his hand. I accepted his apology but did not give him my hand.

The trustee wasn't important. He was already part of the past. I kept thinking of the scene at the office. Lying on my bunk with my eyes closed, I saw the trembling SS man—a contemptible, frightened coward in his black uniform. For years that uniform had been the symbol of terror. I had seen apprehensive German soldiers during the war (the soldiers, too, were afraid of the SS men), but never a frightened

SS man. I had always thought of them as the strong men, the elite, of a perverted regime. It took me a long time to understand what I had seen: the supermen became cowards the moment they were no longer protected by their guns. They were through.

APPENDIX C

Elie Wiesel's Account of the Liberation of Buchenwald

I had to stay until April eleventh. I have nothing to say of my life during this period. It no longer mattered. After my father's death, nothing could touch me any more.

I was transferred to the children's block, where there were six hundred of us.

The front was drawing nearer.

I spent my days in a state of total idleness. And I had but one desire—to eat. I no longer thought of my father or of my mother.

From time to time I would dream of a drop of soup, of an extra ration of soup. . . .

On April fifth, the wheel of history turned.

It was late in the afternoon. We were standing in the block, waiting for an SS man to come and count us. He was late in coming. Such a delay was unknown till then in the history of Buchenwald. Something must have happened.

Two hours later the loudspeakers sent out an order from the head of the camp: all the Jews must come to the assembly place.

This was the end! Hitler was going to keep his promise.

The children in our block went toward the place. There was nothing else we could do. Gustav, the head of the block, made this clear to us with his truncheon. But on the way we met some prisoners who whispered to us:

"Go back to your block. The Germans are going to shoot you. Go back to your block, and don't move."

We went back to our block. We learned on the way that the camp resistance organization had decided not to abandon the Jews and was going to prevent their being liquidated.

As it was late and there was great upheaval—innumerable Jews

135

had passed themselves off as non-Jews—the head of the camp decided that a general roll call would take place the following day. Everybody would have to be present.

The roll call took place. The head of the camp announced that Buchenwald was to be liquidated. Ten blocks of deportees would be evacuated each day. From this moment, there would be no further distribution of bread and soup. And the evacuation began. Every day, several thousand prisoners went through the camp gate and never came back.

On April tenth, there were still about twenty thousand of us in the camp, including several hundred children. They decided to evacuate us all at once, right on until the evening. Afterward, they were to blow up the camp.

So were massed in the huge assembly square, in rows of five, waiting to see the gate open. Suddenly, the sirens began to wail. An alert! We went back to the blocks. It was too late to evacuate us that evening. The evacuation was postponed again to the following day.

We were tormented with hunger. We had eaten nothing for six days, except a bit of grass or some potato peelings found near the kitchens.

At ten o'clock in the morning the SS scattered through the camp, moving the last victims toward the assembly place.

Then the resistance movement decided to act. Armed men suddenly rose up everywhere. Bursts of firing. Grenades exploding. We children stayed flat on the gound in the block.

The battle did not last long. Toward noon everything was quiet again. The SS had fled and the resistance had taken charge of the running of the camp.

At about six o'clock in the evening, the first American tank stood at the gates of Buchenwald.

Our first act as free men was to throw ourselves onto the provisions. We thought only of that. Not of revenge, not of our families. Nothing but bread.

And even when we were no longer hungry, there was still no one who thought of revenge. On the following day, some of the young men went to Weimar to get some potatoes and clothes—and to sleep with girls. But of revenge, not a sign.

Three days after the liberation of Buchenwald I became very ill with food poisoning. I was transferred to the hospital and spent two weeks between life and death.

One day I was able to get up, after gathering all my strength. I wanted to see myself in the mirror hanging on the opposite wall. I had not seen myself since the ghetto.

From the depths of the mirror, a corpse gazed back at me.

The look in his eyes, as they stared into mine, has never left me.

ANNOTATED BIBLIOGRAPHY

Introduction

The total literature on various aspects of the Holocaust is very large, but only a small portion, even tangentially, deals with any aspect of "liberation." For example, the 42 volumes of the *Trial of the Major War Criminals* as well as the volumes covering the individual camp trials do not contain more than a few snippets concerning liberation itself—the defendants, after all, were not on trial for that. The court records do provide some information on the last days in the camps and also ample information of various plans to kill all prisoners before the arrival of the Allies. There are two dozen or so major studies of the Holocaust, and though all of them contain some information on liberation none deal with the question as such for that obviously was not the major concern of the authors. Even the official military histories have very little useful information. The Russian official history barely mentions the subject, as is true of the Russian Encyclopedia; the British official history for this period is yet to be written; two volumes of the American official history do contain fairly detailed descriptions of the liberation of Buchenwald and Dachau from the military point of view.

The contemporary press is useful in studying immediate reactions, but not a very good source of factual data. Survivor literature is the major source of information on liberation and is supplemented by a few accounts written by the liberators themselves. Every camp now has at least one "big" book devoted to it and in all cases there is a section on liberation—sometimes very useful, sometimes only so-so.

General Works

Almost all the standard works on the Holocaust have some information on liberation, but generally in the form of an afterthought. Reuben Ainzstein, *Jewish Resistance in Nazi-Occupied Europe* (New York, 1974) has a useful section on the liberation of Auschwitz; Yehuda Bauer, *A History of the Holocaust* (New York, 1982) all but ends his account before the liberation; Raul Hilberg, *The Destruction of the European Jews* (Chicago, 1961) contains a substantial amount of information on the last weeks before liberation and the various plans of the Germans for the disposition of the inmates; Martin Brozart, "The Concentration Camps 1933–1944," in *Anatomy of the SS State* (ed. by H. Krausnick, *et al.*) deals with liberation only in passing; Lucy Dawidovicz, *The War Against the Jews* (New York, 1975) provides some useful background; Malcolm Proudfoot, *European Refugees: A Study of Forced Population Movement, 1939–1952* (Evanston, Ill., 1959) is the standard work on the administrative history of the various relief agencies and contains a wealth of statistics; H. Trevor-Roper, *The Last Days of Hitler* (New York, 1947) and John Toland, *The Last 100 Days* (New York, 1965) are two good studies of the last days of the war—one scholarly, one popular, but neither contains any information on the camps; Heine Höhne, *The Order of the Death's Head: The Story of Hitler's SS* (New York, 1970) provides background on the SS; Konnilyn Feig, *Hitler's Death Camps* (New York, 1979) is useful; Gerald Reitlinger, *The Final Solution: The Attempt to Exterminate the Jews of Europe* (New York, 1953) is a bit old but still useful for matters pertaining to liberation; Christopher Browning, *The Final Solution and the German Foreign Office* (New York, 1978) touches on rescue operations; Richard Rubenstein, *The Age of Triage* (New York, 1983) is useful; see also Martin Gilbert, *The Fate of the Jews in Nazi Europe* (London, 1979); Yisrael Gutman and Livia Rothkirchen, eds., *The Catastrophe of European Jewry: Antecedents, History and Reflections* (Jerusalem, 1976) for background; Philip Friedman, *Roads to Extinction: Essays on the Holocaust* (New York, 1980) provides provocative insights on a number of issues which have some bearing on liberation; see also Sarah Gordon, *Hitler, Germans and the Jewish Question* (Princeton, 1980); for maps see Martin Gilbert, *The MacMillan Atlas of the Holocaust* (London, 1982); Jacob Presser, *The Destruction of the Dutch Jews* (New York, 1969), one of a number of studies dealing with the fate of individual communities; Nora Levin, *The Holocaust: The Destructon of European Jewry* (New York, 1968)—I found this quite useful on liberation; Eugene Davidson, *The Trial of the Germans* (New York, 1966) is a good digest of the trials.

Majdanek and Auschwitz

There is no book, scholarly or otherwise, on the liberation of Majdanek. The newspapers, however, gave extensive coverage to the liberation. Also Alexander Werth, *Russia at War* (New York, 1964) has a long section on the camp. The *Polish Black Book* also has substantial information on Majdanek although little on its liberation. Since virtually all the Jews—and most of the other prisoners—had been evacuated to Auschwitz before the arrival of the Russians there are no day books or diaries that shed any particular light on the subject.

Whereas the liberation of Majdanek was well covered in both the Russian and Western press, the liberation of Auschwitz was not reported at all until several months after the Russians took the camp. On the other hand, the number of works both primary and secondary that touch on the liberation of Auschwitz is substantial. Josef Garlinski, *Fighting Auschwitz* (Greenwich, Conn., 1975) is useful on resistance in the last months; Primo Levi, *Survival in Auschwitz* (New York, 1960) is excellent, as is Filip Müller, *Eyewitness Auschwitz: Three Years in the Gas Chambers* (New York, 1979); Martin Gilbert's study *Auschwitz and the Allies* (New York, 1981) is quite the best thing done on British and American attitudes and policies concerning Auschwitz and is marginally useful for the liberation.

Dachau

Dachau is better covered than any other camp in respect to liberation. Michael Selzer, *Deliverance Day: The Last Hours of Dachau* (Philadelphia, 1978) is popular in the sense that it lacks footnotes, bibliography etc., but is based on a large number of interviews and is invaluable for anyone wishing to understand the process of liberation. Even more valuable is Marcus Smith's *The Harrowing Hell* (Albuquerque, 1972), a memoir of one of the first Americans in the camp; it is very detailed, very moving. See also Paul Berben *Dachau 1933–1945: The Official History* (London, 1975); Peter Churchill, *The Spirit in the Cage* (London, 1954)—the author was a relative of Churchill and was one of the "prominents" in the camp. See also Nerin Gun, *The Day of the Americans* (New York, 1966). Leo Schwarz, *The Redeemers: A Saga of the Years 1945–1952* (New York, 1953) is one of the few accounts of the experience of liberated Jews in Bavaria in the months just after the war.

Bergen-Belsen

There is one first-rate scholarly study of Bergen-Belsen: Ederhard Kolb, *Bergen-Belsen* (Hannover, 1962). Kolb writes a long section on liberation and an appendix containing a number of valuable documents. *The Trial of Josef Kramer and Forty-Four Others (The Belsen Trial)* ed., Raymond Phillips (London, 1949) has a great deal of information on the last days from the German side. On medical conditions see W. R. F. Collis, "The Belsen Camp: A Preliminary Report," in *British Medical Journal* (1945). Leslie Hardman, *The Survivors: The Story of the Belsen Remnant* (London, 1958) is an account written by a British army rabbi. Alan Morehead, "Belsen," in *Golden Horizon* ed., Cyril Connelly (London, 1955) gives an account of the impression the liberation made in England. The best account from the British side is by Derrick Sington, *Belsen Uncovered* (London, 1966). Sington was the first British soldier inside the camp.

Buchenwald

Elie Wiesel's *Night* (New York, 1969) is a classic. Walter Bartel, ed., *Buchenwald: Mahnung und Verpflictung* (Berlin, East Germany, 1966) contains a mass of information and includes numerous documents, eyewitness accounts and extracts from books. The emphasis, unfortunately, is primarily on the activities of the communists in the camp and that fact somewhat limits its usefulness. Nevertheless, it is the best thing available and the section on the liberation of the camp is over 100 pages long. Klaus Drobisch, *Widerstand in Buchenwald* (Berlin, East Germany, 1977) is also useful. Christopher Burney, *Dungeon Democracy* (New York, 1946) is excellent on the inner workings of the camp. Eugen Kogon, *The Theory and Practice of Hell* (New York, 1950) is one of the earliest and best survivor accounts.

Mauthausen

There is one very good book on Mauthausen: Evelyn Le Chene, *Mauthausen: History of a Death Camp* (London, 1971) which has a long section on liberation. See also Simon Wiesenthal, *The Murderers Among Us: The Wiesenthal Memoirs* (New York, 1967) for an eyewitness account of the liberation.

Theresienstadt

There is one big book on Theresienstadt: H. G. Adler, *Theresienstadt 1941–1945, Das Anlitz einer Zwangsgemeinschaft* (Tübingen, 1955) which contains a substantial amount of information on liberation. See also Albert Friedlander, *Leo Baeck; Teacher of Theresienstadt* (New York, 1968) on the camp's most illustrious inmate. See also Meyer Levin, *In Search* (New York, 1950) which is a deeply felt memoir by an American Army officer who was one of the few Westerners to visit Theresienstadt after liberation.

The Liberators

The British official history of the Second World War does not yet cover the last months of the war so there is no official account of the liberation of Bergen-Belsen. Rather surprisingly, Bergen-Belsen is not mentioned in Montgomery's memoirs. Two volumes in the American historical series are particularly useful: Earl Ziemke, *The U.S. Army in the Occupation of Germany 1944–1946* (Washington, D.C., 1975) and Charles MacDonald, *The Last Offensive* (Washington, D.C. 1973). In addition, Eisenhower's *Papers* contain a substantial amount of information about liberation, which in the last weeks of the war was a matter of major concern at SHAEF. Various divisional histories are also useful. They are often based on "After-Action Reports" which are a mine of information about immediate attitudes and responses to the camps.

Conclusion

I do not think it unreasonable to end an annotated bibliography on the subject of the liberation of the camps with some remarks about the books that do not exist. There is no substantial study of the last weeks before liberation and there is no study that deals with the first weeks after liberation. There is no major study of the death marches; nor of the Red Cross in the last months of the war; nor a military history of liberation. Even the curious story of Himmler's role in the rescue operations is not covered as well as one might have hoped in the standard biographies of the man.

INDEX

Soviet prisoners
  at Dachau at liberation 66
  participating in May Day celebration at Buchenwald 83
  refusing to be repatriated 71
  repatriated former Displaced Persons 71
Soviet Union
  camp liberations not acknowledged in 111
  covering Majdanek story 19
  government failing to publicize Auschwitz atrocities 26–27
  monuments to "victims of fascism" omitting mention of Jews 110
  treatment of Jews in 109
Spanish Jews 37
Spanish loyalists, banner of (illus., #1)
Spectator, editorial on meaning of Bergen-Belsen (quoted 33)
Spottiswoode, Col. —, British army officer
  addressing German civilians at prisoner gravesite (quoted 54–55)
  attending ceremonial burning of Bergen-Belsen camp 56
SS
  abandoning Buchenwald 81
  as loyal followers of Hitler 13
  deaths at gates of Dachau in battle with American Army 66, 75, (fn 6)
  declining authority of during pre-liberation 10
  defiance of by Jews at Buchenwald 81
  departing from Dachau 65
  disarming of at Mauthausen 89, 92
  Economic Administration Office of 29
  evacuation attempts at Majdanek 18
  guards ordered to leave Bergen-Belsen 49
  indirect responsibility for epidemics 10
  pursuit of by former prisoners at Buchenwald 82
  relationship with prisoners during pre-liberation 10
  role in survival of some Jews 13
  transferring control of Theresien-

stadt by 11
SS Panzer Training School, as site of Europe's "last shtetl," 34
Stalbe, Heinz, Majdanek camp official 18
Stalin, J.
  basis of anti-semitic views of 111–112
  demanding compulsory repatriation of prisoners 70
  Eisenhower message to on secondary advance plan 61
  guilty of deaths of Jews 109
  no public mention of Jews by 111
  Silesia as military objective for 26
  views toward prisoners of war 26
Sternlager prisoners 37
  transfer of before liberation 53
Stevens, —, British agent/prisoner 65
Stevens, George, Dachau memorial service filmed by 70
Stone masons, Jewish 78
Stutthof camp 27–28
  date of liberation 30, (fn 1)
  deaths at 27
  German evacuation of 27
  massacre survivors 28
  origins of victims held 27
Supreme Headquarters, Allied Expeditionary Forces (SHAEF) 12
  Displaced Persons Executive (DPX) in 12
  frustrations over refugee problems 11
  policies in dealing with displaced persons problem 67
  rumors of prisoner liquidation received at 64
Swedish Red Cross. See also International Red Cross, Swiss Red Cross
  prisoners at Theresienstadt released to 97
  role in saving lives during pre-liberation 13
Swiss Red Cross. See also International Red Cross, Swedish Red Cross
  role in release of some Theresienstadt prisoners 96
Switzerland
  ransoming of Jews held in Germany 38, 59, (fn 20)

156

Indexed by Phil Roberts,
Nov. 17, 1989